HOPE

FOR MY HOMETOWN

church planting principles from
our journey of faith

DAVE TEIS

First published in 2012 by Striving Together Publications, a ministry of Lancaster Baptist Church, Lancaster, CA 93535. Striving Together Publications is committed to providing tried, trusted, and proven books that will further equip local churches to carry out the Great Commission. Your comments and suggestions are valued.

Striving Together Publications
4020 E. Lancaster Blvd.
Lancaster, CA 93535
800.201.7748

Cover design by Andrew Hutchens
Layout by Beth Lee
Edited by Sarah Browning
Special thanks to our proofreaders

The author and publication team have put forth every effort to give proper credit to quotes and thoughts that are not original with the author. It is not our intent to claim originality with any quote or thought that could not readily be tied to an original source.

ISBN 978-1-59894-200-2

Printed in the United States of America

DEDICATION

I dedicate this book to my wife and children.

Anna, my wife, has stood by me without reservation for these last thirty-five years. She has shared my dreams, along with my ups and downs, my defeats and victories. Whatever has been accomplished in my ministry has been achieved with Anna at my side working tirelessly. She is the one who has stayed with me through every trial and every blessing. She is my inspiration. Anna, I love you because of your faithfulness to Christ, your faithfulness to me and our children, and your commitment to do what is right no matter what obstacles get in the way. The beauty that I behold in your eyes is only a reflection of the inward loveliness that is you.

Our five children have been a blessing to us and our ministry. Matthew, Joshua, Charity, Faith, and Hope are the kind of children a pastor prays for when he considers 1 Timothy 3:4. Moreover, all have a heart for Christ. My sons are both serving as pastors, and all three girls are serving the Lord.

Contents

ACKNOWLEDGMENTS

I give praise and thanks to my Lord and Saviour Jesus Christ for having laid on my heart the desire to write this book.

This work would not have been possible without the help of so many dear friends. I thank God for my many spiritual mentors, including Dr. C. Sumner Wemp, Dr. Don Carter, Dr. Woodrow Kroll, Dr. Dan Mitchell, Ed Hinson, and Earl Miller. These very special men encouraged me and gave me the tools needed to start a New Testament Baptist church in Las Vegas, Nevada.

I also thank the members and friends of Liberty Baptist Church, some of whom have supported this ministry for more than thirty years. It is truly God's church, but the Lord has used many dedicated members to faithfully pray for, give to, and serve at Liberty Baptist Church.

FOREWORD

We were privileged to grow up in the home of gifted church planters and loving parents. Mom and Dad were completely committed to the idea of God raising up a disciple-making church in "Sin City"—a place that would reach the lost souls with the good news of Jesus Christ and be a hub that would send out church plants throughout all the world. We, their five children, consider the church plant of Liberty and its subsequent missionary endeavors to be the second great accomplishment of our parents' lives. What is their greatest accomplishment you might ask? Simply answered, their five incredibly wonderful children—Matthew, Joshua, Charity, Faith, and Hope. Seriously, we're amazing!

The truth is that David and Anna Teis poured into our hearts a love for the work of God, the people of God, and most importantly the person of Jesus Christ. Repeatedly, we have heard our parents speak of the love of God and our responsibility to share that love with the world around us. Many nights we would walk in on my father as he was lying prostrate on the ground in his study in prayer. It was commonplace to catch my mother on the phone in her bedroom counseling some dear lost woman for hours. Again and again, we saw a love for God that expressed itself in a work for God. It formed who we are.

Yes, there were times of difficulty. Yes, if you are attempting to avoid hardship, then church planting is not for you. (I suggest King-Crab fishing in the Bering Sea; I've heard it can be much easier.) There were times that we went months without being paid, but we didn't care because it was fun to have popcorn for dinner. There were times that our clothes came from the missionary barrel and our Christmas came from the Pick-n-Save, but we (the children) never noticed because our parents remained so positive.

Perhaps this seems like an overstatement, but let me assure you it is not. We felt the difficulties, but we never felt the pain. Not only were there financial pressures, but I can remember theological and philosophical pressures. As a church planter everyone wants to mold you into the image of some other man and some other ministry. Once my father told us of a week in which one family told him they were leaving our church because he was too liberal and the very next day a family left our church because we were too conservative. The difficulties of church planting were definitely there, but the joys far outweighed the sorrows. Being in a church planter's family was fun because my parents made it that way. When a new family came to the church, we as a family rejoiced. When the church broke a new growth barrier, we as a family celebrated. And when souls would come to know Christ as Saviour, my parents would share this joy with our entire family.

Life was fun! Disneyland became our family getaway. While thousands of preachers boycotted Mickey and friends, we would pack our little Ford Fiesta and drive the four hours to Anaheim and hang out with the family! To this day we still find time to get Grandma and Grandpa and all of the grandkids down to "our" little getaway in Southern California. We would go camping, go to yard sales, and when a missionary would come to town we would even go out to dinner at Denny's. This is where we, the five, learned to love missionaries and church planters.

Church planters and missionaries were held as the heroes of our home. And although our parents insisted that we follow God's plan for our lives and only enter "full-time" ministry under the direct calling of God, I began to feel the desire to plant and nurture a church from conception to maturity just as I saw my parents do. I am now the pastor of Southern Hills Baptist Church of Las Vegas, and we are currently entering into our eighth year of ministry. Heather and I planted this church under the authority of

Liberty Baptist Church and under the ministry of my dear father. We have seen hundreds come to know Christ as Saviour, and as of this writing we are averaging 450 people in our Sunday morning services. To God be the glory!

We pray this story will encourage you to love Jesus, dream big, and plant more churches in a world that desperately needs the truth.

Pastor Joshua Teis

May 2012

www.shbaptist.com

INTRODUCTION

In 1977, I was about to graduate from Liberty Baptist College in Lynchburg, Virginia. I was not quite twenty-two years old, and I had been encouraged by my professors and mentors to walk by faith and believe God for big things. I was taught that success comes in finding God's will early on in life, and in staying in God's will for all your life. I wanted to do the will of God.

I was in a college that was started out of an independent Baptist church. A young man had graduated from Baptist Bible College and returned to his hometown to plant a church. That young man was Jerry Falwell, and that church became Thomas Road Baptist Church. We were challenged over and over as a student body to consider returning to our hometowns to do what Dr. Falwell had done in his. Although I did not concur with every decision of Dr. Falwell's later ministry, I will forever be indebted to him for challenging me to dream big for God.

However, when I began to tell people of my desire to leave Lynchburg, Virginia, and plant an independent Baptist church in my hometown, people began to caution me. You see, my hometown is Las Vegas, Nevada—"Sin City"—and even back then its reputation was wild. "You can't just graduate from college and go start a church, especially in Las Vegas," I was told by one concerned friend. Another said, "You can't start an independent fundamental Baptist church in Las Vegas. That city can't support a church like that." I even had the privilege of sitting down with Dr. Falwell and sharing with him what I was planning to do. He cautioned me, saying there was already one independent Baptist church in Las Vegas, and he didn't know if the city could sustain two. Yet, God had burdened my heart for my hometown and after graduation in May of 1977, with the complete confidence that God had called us to Las Vegas to start a church, my new bride and I headed out across the United States to start what has become Liberty Baptist Church, here in Las Vegas.

At this writing our church is in its thirty-fifth year, and God has blessed it tremendously. Liberty Baptist Church is proving itself to be God's church here in the Las Vegas Valley. This book is not a "how-to manual." It is the story of two churches that were planted in the Las Vegas Valley and how a church planting strategy was developed. It is written in an autobiographical fashion to be an encouragement to others who may be going through the same struggles we experienced here in "Sin City."

Planting a church is one of the most exhausting and yet rewarding experiences that anyone will ever be called to do. If you are not called to plant a church, I would definitely avoid the task, but if you are called to plant a church, there is nothing more rewarding than watching God use your life to build His church from nothing.

Writing this book has allowed me the opportunity to look back at what God has done over the last thirty-five years. He did not do what I thought He would do, and He did not do it in the fashion I thought He would do it; but He has certainly built something here that only He could have built. So, the name of Jesus Christ gets all the glory for what is happening here in His church and other churches now established in this valley of sin. It's my prayer that this story and the practical applications will inspire, encourage, and instruct you. May God bless you.

PART ONE
A Church Plant in Vegas

ONE

Begin with the End in Mind

I had been on my knees for almost three hours. Everything was uncertain. I had given up my comfortable position as a youth director in a thriving church in North Carolina. Within a month, I would graduate from college. And ten days after graduation, I would marry a beautiful young lady who had agreed to be my wife. I knew in my heart God wanted me to return to my hometown, Las Vegas, Nevada, and begin an independent, fundamental, Bible-believing, Baptist church. As the time to leave the security of my youth pastorate approached, I wondered how it could be accomplished.

Many questions raced through my mind. How would we get to Las Vegas? Where would my new bride and I live? Where would this new church meet? How would we convince people to come? Where would we get the finances we needed? Was this really God's will, or was it only my dream? I was told a person can't graduate from Bible college and immediately start a church. With all of these questions and more attacking my mind, I got on my knees at 9:00 PM, bent over my bed, and began to cry out to God. "Lord, if I'm going to take my new bride to Las Vegas and start a church, I need to have somewhere to live and someplace to meet. I don't know how I'm going to do it, Lord, but You have to at least give me a place to live or someplace to meet." The prayer was not well framed. I did not attempt to impress God with my oratory skills. I simply fell across my bed on bended knees, asking God—often in a semi-conscious state—to please give me a place to meet or a place to live in Las Vegas. I stayed in that position so long that I fell asleep.

I was startled awake by a ringing telephone. I glanced at the clock. I wondered who could be calling so late. My legs had fallen asleep from kneeling so long, but I was finally able to get to the phone.

"David? David, is that you?" the voice asked impatiently.

"Yeah," I answered groggily. "Who is this?"

"It's Al Whalen." (Al was a dear friend from my home church, Gateway Baptist Church in Las Vegas.)

"Al! It's good to hear your voice." I was beginning to wake up. "But why are you calling at midnight?" I asked.

"Oh! I'm sorry," he replied. "I forgot about the time change, but I have some great news, and I knew you would want to hear it."

"Great news?" I thought. "I could use some of that!" "What great news?" I asked.

"I just came from a trustees meeting at our church. Do you know what the topic of discussion was?"

"No, Al. What was it?"

"It was you!" he replied excitedly. "For the entire three hours, we talked about you. We know you want to return to Las Vegas to start a church, and we want to help."

His reply puzzled me. I was unaware that anyone in his church knew my plans.

"We were praying about what we could do to help," he continued. "After a lot of discussion, we agreed that we would either rent a place for you to live or a place to meet. We couldn't decide which, so we decided to leave that decision to you."

I was now fully awake. "Praise the Lord!" I replied. "This is an answer to prayer. Thank you. Thank you so much!"

All I could do was thank God. The Lord orchestrated a trustees meeting 2,500 miles and three time zones away to answer my prayer.

Though this was the beginning of the material provision for the church I wanted to start in Las Vegas, it was not the spiritual beginning. If I were asked, "Where did Liberty Baptist Church start?" I would reply that it began as a God-given desire placed in the heart of a seventeen-year-old boy.

MY STORY

I grew up in church. My father passed away when I was only ten, and my mother made sure I was in church every Sunday morning and evening and Wednesday night. I knew about Jesus. I knew it was right to go to church. And I wanted to do right, but like every man since Adam, I often found my flesh struggling against my spirit.

At the age of sixteen, I heard a message by Evangelist David Wilkerson on the Second Coming of Jesus Christ. I determined that I was going to live for Christ and do everything I could to tell lost people about His saving power. Soon after this I began to attend Gateway Baptist Church in Las Vegas, a relatively young church. A dynamic, young preacher who was on fire for the Lord pastored the church. And it was there that some very dear, fundamental Baptist families encouraged me to serve the Lord with my whole heart.

As I attempted to follow their advice, I faced the struggle of obedience to God and, at the same time, negative peer pressure from my public school classmates at Rancho High School. They mocked the idea of my serving the Lord. I was soon labeled "the preacher" because I would carry my Bible to school to encourage myself to do the right thing.

I began to dream of someday starting a Christian school in the Las Vegas Valley that would compete with the other schools—a Christian school where peer pressure would encourage students to do right instead of wrong. This desire led me to enroll in Lynchburg

Baptist College (later Liberty Baptist College and later Liberty University) which had recently been started by Dr. Jerry Falwell.

The college had been started out of a local church. The professors emphasized the importance of establishing independent, fundamental Baptist churches. No matter which courses I took, the emphasis was on leading people to Jesus Christ and getting them involved in a local church. They warned against assuming some old, dead church and encouraged us to plant new churches. Dr. Falwell had gone back to his hometown to start a church, and we were encouraged to do the same. We were told it was easier to birth a baby than raise the dead.

During my first year of college, I became concerned that I had never truly trusted Christ as my Lord and Saviour. After hearing a stirring message from J. Harold Smith entitled "God's Three Deadlines" and another by evangelist Del Fehsenfeld, Jr. called "Phony Bologna Christians," I came forward and met a young man named Scott Payne. He led me in prayer as I bowed my head and made my salvation sure. (It is because of my experience that today at Liberty Baptist Church we ensure that everyone who comes forward to join our church is questioned in detail about his or her salvation experience. We want people to know for sure they are going to Heaven.)

Following my sophomore year in college, I was invited to work in a summer program, along with three other Christian college students. I spent that summer knocking on doors and inviting people to come to church. That fall, as a result of working in that program, I was invited to help start an independent Baptist church in Burlington, North Carolina, under the leadership of Pastor Donald Carter, and I was soon helping with the youth of his church on the weekends during my junior and senior years of college.

In January of 1977, while I continued to work in Burlington, I began to develop a burden for the people of my hometown. I started to seek God's face about the need for a new Baptist church in Las Vegas. Burlington was only two hours away from the college campus, and I was content with the job I was doing there. I intended to continue my work with the youth department until the Lord gave me new direction.

Having been taught from the Word of God that God uses authorities in our lives to give us direction, I asked the Lord that if He wanted me to return to Las Vegas and start a church, that He would use my God-given authorities to direct me. I believe very strongly in parental and pastoral authority. Since my father had died, my mother was my authority. My fiancé Anna was in much the same situation, under her mother's authority. I was also under Dr. Carter's pastoral authority at Burlington. Having told my mother, Anna's mother, and Dr. Carter of the situation, I wondered if it would be God's will for me to return to Las Vegas or remain in Burlington.

I asked the Lord to make His desire for my life clear and to let me know His will through those three authorities. Shortly after praying that prayer, Anna's mother contacted her. She told Anna she believed it was God's will for us to move to Las Vegas where we would start a church. My mother assured me of the same thing. Yet, I had still not heard from Dr. Carter.

I had found security in my position under Dr. Carter in Burlington. I thought I was doing a good job with the church's young people, and if it wasn't God's will that I plant a church in Las Vegas, I rationalized that at least I would be serving Him as youth director in Dr. Carter's church.

One Saturday I walked into the pastor's office to brief him on a six-month plan for our youth ministry. Before I could launch into my presentation, he said to me, "Brother Dave, before we discuss anything else, I need to share with you something that God has put on my heart. I do not believe that you are going to be content here. In fact, I believe you are not going to be content until you go to Nevada and start a church."

His remark took me by surprise. Yet, as soon as he said it, a burden was lifted from my spirit. I told him of the commitment I had made to God concerning input from three authorities, and then we discussed my going to Las Vegas.

After I left Dr. Carter's office, I met Anna in the parking lot. I told her excitedly that we were going to Las Vegas to start a church. Anna smiled and nodded in agreement. We had no promise of material provision. We knew nothing of deputation and, if we had, we wouldn't have had anyone to look to for support. We did not have great faith, we just knew this was God's leading. He had made His will clear through our God-given authorities. God was teaching me that it does not take great faith to start a church, just a little faith in a great God.

Anna and I made a prayer list of things we needed and wanted to start our ministry. We began to pray daily that God would supply all our needs. I have that prayer list to this day. It is scribbled on a page in the prayer journal I was using at the time. Between the time we created it and the day that I got on my knees and thanked God for His provision, we saw Him provide one needed thing after another, one step at a time.

PREPARING TO PLANT A CHURCH

Over the last thirty-five years, we have watched many people attempt to plant independent Baptist churches. We have watched a few independent Baptist churches compromise with the world. We have watched some begin and have seen some fold. I have learned from my experience that there are some essentials for anyone who desires to start an independent Baptist church.

If you desire to plant a church, be sure that your desire is a God-given desire. Psalm 37:4 says, "Delight thyself also in the LORD; and he shall give thee the desires of thine heart."

Make sure you are walking with God daily and loving Him simply for who He is. Reading His Word, praying, and winning others to Christ confirm your walk with Him. If you are doing God's will, He will place desires in your heart that He intends to fulfill.

Seek God's direction through God-given authorities. Ask those who are in positions of authority over you if they believe planting a church is God's will for you. Ask them to pray about it and then give their opinions. Let God open the door—don't force it. A door that is pried open will be left open when you want to leave. A door that God opens will be gently closed by our loving Saviour to keep you where He wants you.

Make sure you know what you believe and believe what you know to be God's Word. Be grounded in the principles of Scripture and ready to share and defend your faith based upon the Word of God.

Be willing to work long and hard without much positive human recognition, but with MUCH human criticism. I was criticized by people I did not know, as well as by those who were close to me. The Bible tells us in 1 Corinthians 2:15, "But he that is spiritual judgeth all things, yet he himself is judged of no man." Some do not understand the reasoning of a man who is walking in the Spirit.

Finally, be sure you are willing to stick it out for the long haul. A mushroom pops up overnight, but a huge oak tree takes a lifetime to grow. Plant an oak, not a mushroom. Liberty Baptist Church is thirty-five years old, but in so many ways, we've only just begun.

TWO

And So It Starts

O n May 10, 1977, Anna and I graduated from Bible college. On May 11, we, along with Anna's mother (who had come for graduation), packed our baby blue 1973 Torino Station Wagon and hit the road. We began a two-day trip over the Blue Ridge Parkway to Brookville, Pennsylvania, where Anna had been raised. Ten days later, on May 21, 1977, at 1:00 PM on a cool spring day, Anna and I stood under the shade of a beautiful pine tree next to a creek in her mother's backyard and exchanged wedding vows.

My pastor, Dr. Don Carter, his wife and family, and many church members and dear friends from North Carolina attended the ceremony. After a week-long honeymoon traveling through eastern Virginia, historic Jamestown, Williamsburg, and Jefferson's home, Monticello, we returned to Lynchburg to finish one last class I needed for graduation. (I graduated with an asterisk next to my name which meant, in order to get my diploma, I needed to retake English Literature. I mention that only to encourage those reading this that God does use the gifted, as well as the not-so-gifted.)

The course concluded at the end of June, and on July 1, 1977, Anna and I left for Las Vegas with $25 in our pockets. Someone had graciously purchased a moving trailer for our use, and we stayed with friends and relatives as we made our way West. Many had given us money for graduation and wedding gifts, and those carried us all the way to Omaha, Nebraska. When the money ran out, I called my mother to ask if we had any money in the bank. "Five hundred dollars," she replied. I asked her to send some so we could travel the rest of the way to our new home. Finally, on July 10, 1977, we pulled into Las Vegas, Nevada.

The Lord provided a trailer for us to live in for an incredible $100 a month. We were given only three months to stay in that trailer. Towards the end of the three months, through a man we met doorknocking, God miraculously provided a house for rent exactly within our price range.

Even in those first moments of moving back to Las Vegas, God was graciously providing for us. We had a place to live and a place to meet. Gateway Baptist Church had rented a meeting room in a private school building on the southwest side of Las Vegas, and shortly after arriving, I met with Pastor Duane Pettipiece of Gateway. He interviewed me to determine whether or not I was a "real" Baptist. He asked several questions, and after convincing himself, he told me that he had something to show me.

We jumped into his car and drove across town to a mini-storage warehouse. As mentioned previously, Anna and I had created a prayer list of things we needed to start a church. The list included items such as a sound system, hymnals, a piano, and other things we felt would be necessary or helpful to start a church.

My chin hit the ground when Pastor Pittipiece swung open the doors to the storage unit. I felt like I was a contestant on The Price is Right. And the price was right!

"Several months ago there was a church here in Las Vegas that closed its doors." He began to tell me, "When they heard you were coming to Las Vegas to start a church, they entrusted us with these things to deliver to you. There are one hundred folding chairs, a good sound system, some fairly new hymnals, and all the materials you will need for a children's church and Sunday school program." There in that storage unit was virtually every material thing Anna and I had been praying for.

"Oh," Pastor Pettipiece added. "Before I forget to tell you, we also have a pretty good piano. We're keeping it for you at a member's house."

"You've given us everything Anna and I had on our prayer list," I said. "Thank you. Thank you so much!" It was amazing to see how God heard and answered our prayers.

And so began the start of our church—Liberty Baptist Church. When deciding what we would name the church, people have asked why we chose Liberty Baptist Church. Some may think we chose the name out of a sincere loyalty to Liberty Baptist College. And although I am very grateful for the fact that Dr. Falwell started Liberty and for the great training we received there, the main reason we chose that name was because we could use their artwork. They had artwork that said, "Liberty Baptist" and "LBC." At that time, we had no access to a personal computer, and when you talked about putting together a flyer, you literally did "cut and paste." My wife and I used old issues of the Sword of the Lord, college magazines and other materials to create a flyer that we could take to Postal Instant Press (a quick copy company). We printed hundreds of flyers to distribute. The flyer was an 8½ x 11-inch tri-fold. Our goal was to distribute at least one hundred flyers every afternoon between then and our first Sunday service scheduled for September 11th.

With flyers in hand, Anna and I hit the pavement in the 110-degree July heat. We wanted to make a good impression on the people who answered their door, and so we were dressed to the hilt (for me, that meant a dark suit and tie; and for Anna, a dress, high-heels, and nylons). We realized we weren't much more than two kids playing dress-up in the flesh, but our spirits were doing anything

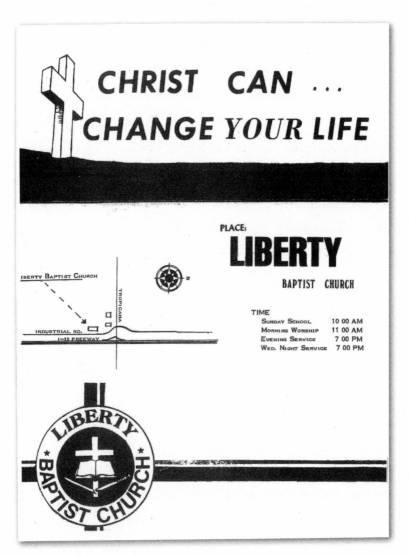

First church flyer

but playing. Anna and I were totally committed to the Lord and to starting Liberty Baptist Church. Whenever people would express even a hint of interest in what we had to say, I pulled out a small notebook and copied down their names and phone numbers.

We knocked on doors from that July until early September. Two couples had made commitments to attend the first Sunday service, Mr. and Mrs. Larry Sample and Mr. and Mrs. Dave Alons. Dave was a member of Gateway Baptist Church and had been my counselor at teen camp when I was sixteen. Larry was an older man who lived in the southwest part of town. He had been hoping a good Bible-teaching church would be planted in that area. Larry also had a big yellow and white trailer he let us use to haul chairs and other equipment back and forth to the rented schoolroom we were using for services. The Saturday evening before the Big Day, we set up the rented room for the next morning's service.

We established a somewhat limited organizational structure. Anna would be the junior church and Sunday school teacher. Dave and Larry would serve as ushers, and Dave's wife would run the nursery.

Sunday morning, September 11th, finally dawned. Perhaps dawned is not the most accurate description. Anna and I awoke to the sound of cracking thunder and huge raindrops splattering on our trailer's metal roof. Las Vegas gets only about 6 inches of rain a year, and it generally comes in one day. I was concerned. Anna and

I had been working our fingers to the bone for the last two months to make sure everything was ready for the Big Day.

At first I began to question God. "Why, Lord? Why must it rain on this day of all days?" I whined. "We've worked so hard!" We had even sent letters to prospective attendees and called them every week to remind them of their commitment to attend our first service. We had been praying for 150 people to come that first Sunday. We did not know how many would attend because of the rain. Our college taught us to think BIG—and now we had this big, horrible storm.

At the conclusion of my complaining to God, I remembered whose church and rain it really was. I remembered that God is in control. We had done everything we could, and the results were up to Him. We continued to pray, but the rain just kept coming. The lesson I realized later was that it's God who determines how many will attend church, not the weather.

Even though the sky was still liquid when the service began, we had sixty-eight people come to our first Sunday service. God had also been good in providing us with a young couple. The young man was a pianist, and while he played the piano, I led the music, gave the announcements and preached. I preached a message entitled "You Can Know for Sure You're Going to Heaven." Two people responded to the altar call and trusted Jesus Christ as their Lord and Saviour. I walked into the little foyer, shut the door so no one could see me, and jumped up and down with joy.

Dear Friend,

I would like to personally invite you to attend Liberty Baptist Church. Liberty Baptist Church is a Fundamental, Bible believing Church that is interested in you. Christ has a plan for you as an individual. He is concerned about you in a personal way. He has provided for you a way to have everlasting and abundant life. Abundant life is life with a purpose, and you can find this life through His Son.

Please come and be with us at Liberty Baptist Church. I would like to meet you personally and share with you all that Christ has done for me and can do for you.

Pastor Dave Teis

WHY – LIBERTY BAPTIST CHURCH?

1. Every minute 87 people die and go to Hell. This is not just a calculated guess; this is a fact. Many of these people die without ever realizing that through Christ they could know for sure that they have a home in Heaven. They have never been told the secret of eternal life that is outlined in the Bible. Christ established the local Church for this purpose.

2. Everyone in life is hunting for a purpose. Many live for wealth, others for popularity, others for fame. However, the Bible declares "all these things shall pass away." There is, however, a way to find true purpose in life. Christ established the fundamental local Church to show man this purpose.

Letter that was sent out to prospective attendees

That first Sunday morning, while I was busy teaching adults, we had also planned an exciting children's Sunday school program and a nursery. Several weeks before our church doors opened, Anna and I had constructed and painted several puppet stages to use for our children's church ministry. We also collected several CEF (Child Evangelism Fellowship) Bible and missionary storybooks so that we could have a variety of activities for all the children that attended on our opening day. As junior church began, we put on exciting children's sing-along tapes so that the children would have a fun atmosphere as they came into church. Miss Anna, as the children affectionately knew her, then led the children in songs and introduced the children to our puppet friends who basically moved their mouths to pre-recorded songs that we had practiced the week before. Dave Alons, one of our ushers, also served as our "Puppet Master." After the show, Anna taught an exciting flannelgraph lesson. All the programs were simple but exciting! Liberty Baptist Church had become a reality.

The following Sunday, we had 48 people in our service. On our third Sunday, we had 43, and on our fourth Sunday, we had only 34. During each service, as I preached on faith in God, I wondered what God was doing with His new church. The room appeared nearly empty from the makeshift pulpit. But, on that low day, God did something miraculous to remind us that He was still in charge. We received an offering of over $1,300! That doesn't sound like much today, but up to that point, our highest offering had been $268, which we received on our first Sunday.

As we took the offering on that first Sunday, I had told those attending that we were taking an offering because my wife and I had $14 in the bank, and if we didn't have a good offering we wouldn't eat that week. That Sunday we had our highest attendance but our smallest offering. On our fourth Sunday, with our lowest attendance, God gave us over $1,300. God was opening the windows of Heaven for us.

Though Anna and I worked very hard day after day knocking on doors, preparing lessons, doing follow-up work and counseling, neither of us has had to work a secular job to support the church or ourselves. God provided as we poured our lives into His work.

Liberty Baptist Church still operates the same way today. The only difference is that back then we prayed for a $250 weekly offering; now, with about 1,100 members, we pray for $50,000 a week. Jesus said, "When you pray, say, 'Give us this day our daily bread.'" I have found through the years that this is exactly how God answers prayers. Day by day, He gives us what He knows we need.

On that fourth Sunday, Anna and I discussed what the $1,300 offering should be used for. One option we considered was to deposit it and use it later for weeks when the collections were anemic. Our decision, however, was to use the money to advertise our new church.

Dr. Falwell had a weekly television show titled "The Old Time Gospel Hour" on Sunday mornings. Dr. Falwell's show aired in Las Vegas hours before our service started. We purchased a series of one-minute spots on the local affiliate following his weekly broadcast. I went on the air and explained that my name was Dave Teis, that we had started a new church called Liberty Baptist Church, that I was a recent graduate of Dr. Falwell's college, and that if the viewers wanted a church like Dr. Falwell's here in the Las Vegas Valley, they should come to Liberty. Several new families visited the church as a result of those ads, and our attendance began to grow. The schoolroom that had seemed so big and so empty those first few weeks now seemed crowded. After only six months, it became apparent that we needed more room.

I asked the landlord if she would allow us to expand into more space. We needed double the size we were currently renting, I explained. She was surprised that we had grown so fast. I thought perhaps she would double the rent from $200 a month to $400. She told me that we could double our space, but that the rent would be $1,000 a month. That's when I began to understand what my math teacher meant by "exponential"! Prayerfully, I decided that we should not have to pay that kind of money to use a room once a week.

Soon after, we found a warehouse in an industrial area of the city. A very gracious gentleman owned the building. He told us we could rent it on a permanent basis. A further blessing was that we would not have to move equipment in and out every week. The rent would be no more than we would be paying for the schoolroom: $1,000 a month. It made more sense paying $1,000 a month for a building we could use every day than for only four days a month. Being poor, but not stupid, we took the offer.

We used that building for over two years. It was wonderful how God blessed His church during that time. On our second anniversary, we had a special singing group in town called Light Ministries and a high attendance of 210. Things were going well; however, between our second and third anniversary, things took a turn for the worse.

Las Vegas is a very transient city. Many people move in every month, while a large number move out. That year was a big downturn for our membership. A few things contributed to the downturn. People moved because of job losses in the valley and employment opportunities elsewhere. Some of our members left because they felt called into full-time Christian ministry. Two of the families that made up our entire Sunday school staff moved to California to work at a Christian camp. Another new church opened in town and some left Liberty to graciously help that church get started. Our landlord sold the warehouse, and many, thinking we would no longer have a place to meet, started attending other churches—some with questionable doctrine.

As we approached our third anniversary, we faced a time of real discouragement. We were about to lose our meeting place, and our weekly attendance had contracted to about fifty. Nevertheless, Anna and I still believed that God had called us to Las Vegas and that it didn't matter how many people were in weekly services. This is where God had called us to be and, until further direction, this is where we would stay.

About a week before we had to move out of our rented warehouse, a lady named Mary Jane Hitter, one of our earliest members, called about a vacant dance studio near her home. It was located on a main thoroughfare. Anna and I looked at the building, and we agreed that it would be perfect to help us get our ministry back on track. We had very limited funds, so I called up the real estate agent and expressed an interest. I informed him that we could only afford what we had been paying for the warehouse. He said he didn't think the owner would accept such a low offer; however, when he approached the man who owned the building, he graciously accepted our bid.

Within a week's time, we moved into the dance studio and transformed it into an independent Baptist church! With the loss of some of our previous members to some questionable denominations came the realization that we needed to disciple our members so they would understand what we believe and why all churches are not alike.

We spent the next ten years in the converted dance studio teaching our members the Bible verse by verse. We put any further building plans aside and concentrated on teaching the people God's

Word and where their church stood on the doctrinal teachings contained within the Scriptures.

God blessed our ministry as we steadfastly taught His Word to His people. Within eight years, our services were running around 250 on regular Sundays and about 300 on Christmas and Resurrection Sunday. It soon became apparent that we needed to find a permanent location, a base from which we could reach the entire city. God had put on our hearts to establish a K5–12th grade Christian School. And we knew that having a base could help us plant other churches in the Las Vegas Valley and support missionaries around the world.

THREE

An Unexpected Blessing

Our church had been meeting in rented facilities since its inception in September of 1977. And in 1986, we began to view that as a problem. If we were going to be effective in helping start other churches, we realized we needed our own base of operations.

We began to look for property. Property was very expensive and we did not know of any wealthy people attending our church. Many of the 250–300 attendees were children. A large offering on a given Sunday was around $2,000.

Anna and I began to pray about what God would have us do when it came to purchasing a piece of property. We determined that we would start looking at 2½-acre parcels to see if we could find something reasonable. We also determined that if we could find a desirable piece of property, we would sell our home that God had provided and take the equity and use it as a down payment on the church property. We would move a trailer onto the lot and live in it until such time that we could actually build a church and maybe a parsonage on the property.

The men of the church agreed to our strategy. We found a 2½-acre parcel that was very rough. In fact, there was a huge sinkhole in the middle of the property. No one else was interested in it. However, the price was right: $85,000. Other parcels of similar size were around $120,000. We made an offer to the owner contingent on the county zoning it for our use.

After we put down a small deposit, I got a sinking feeling in my stomach. I thought, "How in the world are we going to raise $85,000?" The answer came from watching "The Old Time Gospel Hour." Dr. Falwell announced that a donor had offered a matching gift for every gift given up to a limit of $5 million. He explained that if someone gave a dollar to Liberty Baptist College, it would be matched by the donor so it was like giving $2. If one gave $10, the college would actually receive $20, and so on. I thought, if God could do that for Dr. Falwell for a $5 million need, why couldn't He do it for me? After all, we only needed $85,000. I really didn't pray about it, I just wondered, "Why not?"

The following Sunday I announced to our church that we were going to try to raise money for a piece of property. I explained that we had found a 2½-acre parcel and that Anna and I were going to sell our house and use the money for a down payment. I explained further that we needed to raise $85,000. I asked the members to pray about it. I told them that on a particular Sunday we were going to take an offering after asking God to give us the money we needed to purchase the property. This was the biggest step of faith I had ever taken. This was going to take a miracle from God.

Every Monday, I spent time with my family. It was our Sabbath rest. I have continued this practice to this day. It is the one day that I try to sleep in a little.

It was 7:00 AM Monday morning when the ringing of the phone brought me out of my dreams. "Dave?! Dave, is that you?" he asked.

I recognized the voice. "Yeah, it's me, Mac." Mac was an older gentleman in our church and a bachelor. He had been attending regularly, but he had never understood the importance of joining the church.

"Dave! I need to ask you a question," he said with some urgency. Mac was a likeable enough guy, but he didn't seem to have any friends or relatives. He was a recluse who lived in a one-bedroom apartment.

"What's that, Mac?" I asked. Anna moaned, fluffed her pillow several times, and rolled over with her back toward me.

"Dave, do you really think that little ol' church of yours can raise $85,000?"

I really wasn't in the mood to have my faith or our church questioned at such an early hour. And I didn't like hearing our church referred to as a "little ol' church." However, I wanted to be as gracious as possible.

"Mac," I replied. "I don't believe we can do anything, but I do believe that God can."

"Yeah! But, Dave, do you really think that you can raise $85,000?"

"Mac, I'm just trusting God. I believe God can do anything."

"Well, Dave," Mac continued, "I don't think that church is going to be able to raise $85,000, but I'll tell you what. I'm going to give your church $45,000."

One moment I was half asleep, the next, wide awake. I thought perhaps I had misunderstood. "Did you say, 'Four to five thousand,' Mac?"

"No, Dave," he replied. "You heard me correctly. I said $45,000! I've got some investments that will mature in the next few days, and I intend to give a sizable chunk of that money to your church." I elbowed Anna in the ribs. She ignored me. "If I give $45,000," he continued, "do you think that church of yours can raise the other $40,000?"

I cupped my hand over the mouthpiece and told Anna what Mac had said. She bolted upright in bed. Her eyes grew wide. "Well, yes, Mac," I replied flabbergasted. "I believe the Lord can do that, but, Mac, you're not even a member of our church. Are you sure you want to do this?"

Anna gave me that cocked-head look that only a wife can give when her husband is about to say or do something stupid. "Dave, you're about to blow it," she quietly mouthed. "Keep your mouth shut!" I nodded my head to let her know that I had read her lips successfully.

"Well, Mac, that's wonderful," I said. "So you're going to give the church $45,000 if we can raise the other $40,000," I repeated for Anna's sake. "Well, God bless you, Mac! I'm going to announce that to the church this Sunday."

I hadn't really prayed for this blessing. I just thought, "God, if you can do it for Jerry Falwell, why can't you do it for me?" And God again showed Himself strong. Six weeks later we took that special offering. We collected $14,000 in cash and another $26,000 in pledges. We were ready to buy the property. "Just a few more little details and we can begin construction," or so I thought.

THE POWERS THAT BE

We prove our age with birth certificates. We prove our social security number by showing a small piece of government paper with numbers printed on it. We prove to the police officer that it's our car by showing him a piece of paper most of us carry in the glove compartment called a vehicle registration. Paper, paper everywhere. And it's no different with a piece of real estate. One must have proper documentation confirming property ownership.

Our next step in the paper chase was to get approval from the county to use that 2½-acre parcel to build a church. Anyone who has been involved in getting a permit understands that it takes months and lots of bureaucratic wrangling. In Las Vegas, one has to submit the paperwork to the City Staff. If they approve, then the application goes to the Planning Council for consideration. This usually takes thirty to sixty days.

We were anxious to start the process. We finally got on the Planning Council's agenda, but when we went before the board, much to our surprise, the City Staff recommended against us. They said that the citizens objected to having a church in that area. The Planning Council followed the staff's recommendation and turned us down. We still had one more shot. We would go before the County Commission and plead our case. We lost. The Commission ruled that there were other locations more suitable for a church. We accepted the Commission's decision as from the Lord. Proverbs 21:1 teaches us, "The king's heart is in the hand of the LORD, as the rivers of water: he turneth it whithersoever he will." Romans 13:1–2 exhorts, "Let every soul be subject unto the higher powers. For there is no power but of God: the powers that be are ordained of God. Whosoever therefore resisteth the power, resisteth the ordinance of God...." A part of the rebel within me wanted to fight. However, the Word of God tells us that "the powers that be are ordained of God...." I got together with my associate pastor and Anna and we prayed and thanked God for the situation and interpreted this as His leading us.

The following week I announced to our church that we would be looking for another piece of land because God was directing us elsewhere. At that time, we had pledges for $85,000, but we didn't yet have the property, so I prayed that the people would not get discouraged and that they would keep their promised pledges.

Shortly thereafter, we found another 2½-acre parcel. This one was only $80,000 and the property was on a carrier street, across from a boys club, and ideal for outreach. It was a flat piece of desert property without blemish. It seemed that God had kept us from purchasing the other property, and saved us $5,000 that we could put toward building the church.

We immediately applied for permission to buy the property. Excitement began to build again at Liberty over the possibility of finally moving onto our own property. This time, we got a positive recommendation from the City Staff. The Planning Council also gave us a tentative thumbs up. Things were going so smoothly that Anna and I packed up the family and took a little vacation. We returned just in time to go to the County Commission hearing, anticipating receiving our final approval.

However, the meeting room was filled with local area residents who had come to protest having a church in their neighborhood. Some expressed concern that there would be too much noise at the church and that it would affect their lifestyles. After much discussion, the Commissioners harkened to the concerns of the mob and voted us down.

I tried to get past my first emotional response which was something less than Christian. I kept concentrating on Jesus' words in John 15:18, "If the world hate you, ye know that it hated me before it hated you."

After the meeting, the rebel surfaced again. I said to my associate pastor, Bob Smith, "We should take them to court! We should call the Christian Law Association! They can't stop a church from building! It's against our constitutional rights!" I protested. But Bob reminded me of what I preach—the powers that be are ordained of God. He told me that he believed God was going to give us a better piece of property if we would just be patient and wait on the Lord. Frankly, my patience was wearing thin. We'd been in Las Vegas for ten years in rented facilities. I thought it was time for us to have a place of our own.

It was then that one County Commissioner asked me, "Preacher, would you be willing to meet with the head of our Comprehensive Planning Department? He can show you some sites to build on where no one will object." I agreed to a meeting. The Commissioner continued, "I am tired of turning this preacher down! Help him find a piece of property that he can build a church on."

FOUR

Rewards of Submission

First Peter 2:13–14 teaches, "Submit yourselves to every ordinance of man for the Lord's sake: whether it be to the king, as supreme; Or unto governors, as unto them that are sent by him for the punishment of evildoers, and for the praise of them that do well." I knew Bob was right. I knew, too, that I had to beat back the rebel within if I wanted God's blessing. If we submit to the authorities God has placed in our lives, He will use them to direct us, I thought, just as He did in bringing us to Las Vegas.

The following week, I met with the Comprehensive Planning Director, as suggested by the County Commissioner. He showed me several parcels of available property. These weren't 2½ acres, they were 5, 10, 15 and 20-acre parcels. There is no way we can afford these properties, I thought. He must have read my face because he told me about a federal program by which churches and other non-profit organizations in Nevada can purchase expensive property for only 50% of fair market value. He explained further that, if there was a school attached for educational purposes, the land could be acquired for 10 percent of fair market value.

We made our way to the Director's office where he showed us on a county map several available parcels. Most were so far out in the desert that one would need a four-wheel-drive vehicle to get there. However, there was one piece that looked intriguing. It was on the corner of a major highway that ran through the city. When I asked the Director why he thought that parcel was available, he explained that it must be a mistake. He looked through his records, however, and confirmed that there were no claims on the property. He suggested that I go to the local federal office to see if they had any recorded claims on the property.

When I arrived at the Las Vegas Bureau of Land Management (BLM), I found two helpful bureaucrats. They looked up the property in one of their huge, bound volumes. The pages had yellowed from age. Sam, one of the two, told me there were no claims on the property as far as he could tell. "How do I make application for that property?" I asked. He informed me that the application process would take years.

First, the application would have to be completed. It would have to be accompanied by a five-year property development plan.

The completed application would have to be submitted to the Las Vegas office of the BLM, along with an application fee. The Bureau would examine it for approximately one year. Following this, it would be sent to and evaluated further by the Carson City office, a process that would take six months to a year. After their evaluation, the application would be returned to the Las Vegas office for finalization, which could take between 6 months to a year. The total process could last between 2½ to 3 years.

Two things crossed my mind. First, this piece of property would be excellent. It was large enough to have a base that we could use to reach the entire city. Second, the bad thing was that it was going to take years to process the paperwork and there was no assurance that we would be successful in obtaining the property.

I knew God wanted us to be subject to "the powers that be." I completed the application and the required property development plan. Within a few weeks, I was back at the Las Vegas office of the BLM to submit our application and fee.

The lady at the front desk informed me that the application process had been changed. I was afraid I would have to redo the paper work. She saw my "Oh, no" countenance and laughed. She assured me that the paperwork was okay. She explained the only change was that the application had to be submitted to the Carson City office.

Filing the application in the state capitol might save some time, I thought. Since Carson City is only an eight-hour drive from Vegas,

I thought we'd drive the application to the capitol rather than mail it. Following that next Sunday night service, on a beautiful moonlit night, Anna and I packed up the family and drove to Carson City. We got there as the sun was rising.

Later that morning, I drove to the federal building. I finally found the BLM office and entered through the double glass doors that boasted the agency's logo. A lady asked, "May I help you?"

I explained that I was a pastor in Las Vegas and that we were making application for a piece of BLM property for our church.

"You look a little confused," she said. "Let me see if I can help." She waved me over to a desk and sat down. She appeared to be in her mid-fifties. She looked over the application. "I believe everything is in order," she remarked. She scribbled some notes in the margins. "Well, Reverend Teis," she offered, "I believe I can have this back in the Las Vegas Office within the next two weeks."

My jaw dropped to the floor. A six-month to a one-year process had just been time-shrunk to two weeks. This lady must be an angel, I thought. I could do nothing but praise God for His intervention! God wants us to build His church His way! I thought.

Two weeks later, I walked into the Las Vegas office of the BLM. The woman at the front desk remembered me from my first visit. I asked if my application had come back from Carson City. She assured me with a smile that it hadn't. I returned her smile and asked her to please check anyway.

She looked through the well organized stack of papers on her desk. I wished my desk looked so organized. She looked up at me. Her smile had morphed into a frown. "Huh," she grunted. "It's here." Now the frown turned into a look of disapproval. She removed her glasses and looked up at me. "Reverend Teis," she began in a condescending tone, "I don't know why they processed your application so quickly, but you are going to have to follow the same process everyone else does. We'll get back with you in six months to a year." It's good to have a Friend in high places, I thought!

I knew better than to antagonize a bureaucrat that held the future of my church in her hands. Sometimes paperwork gets misplaced for months or even years. I put on the best smile I could muster, thanked her, and left the office.

Shortly thereafter, the landlord informed us that he had to sell the property that we had been renting for more than eight years, and that we needed to move out quickly.

Knowing that the powers that be are ordained of God, I wrote our Senator a gracious letter and asked if there was any way that he could speed things up. Colossians 4:6 tells us, "Let your speech be alway with grace, seasoned with salt, that ye may know how ye ought to answer every man." I made no demands. I just asked humbly if he could help us get our property sooner.

Within a matter of weeks, I received a phone call from Sam at the Bureau of Land Management's Las Vegas office. He told me that "Senatorial action had been taken" on our property and that he had been instructed to process this application as soon as possible. When I arrived at his office, he told me that our application had been preliminarily approved. There was only one thing left to do and that was to have a formal appraisal made on the property.

There was only one man in the state that conducted appraisals on federal property, according to Sam. He worked in the northern part of the state, as well as the southern. His name was Joe. Sam gave me his number, and I contacted him to find out when he would be in the Las Vegas Valley. He said that it would be several months, but he would come as fast as he could. I thanked him and called him on a weekly basis. We became phone friends. One day he contacted me. He said that he was going to be in Las Vegas and since I had expressed such an intense interest (translated—nagged) he would appraise our property first.

A short time later, Joe called again. "Reverend Teis," he began. "I have my appraisal. While I don't normally give it over the phone, I know you have been waiting a long time (translation—please don't call me again). I've appraised your property at $180,000, so the cost to you would be $90,000, if you buy it for 50% of fair market value."

"$90,000?" I repeated. "That's great! Thanks Joe. Thanks for everything."

As I put the phone down, I thought about God's unfailing sovereignty. We had looked at a 2 ½-acre piece of property just a year or so before that we were going to buy for $85,000. It would have been a costly proposition to build on it. We then looked at another

2½-acre parcel for $80,000. God used the county government to stop us from buying that property. He used them to direct us to the federal agency and, through it, we were going to be able to buy a 17½-acre parcel for only $5,000 more than the original one.

FIVE

God Is Not Finished

We felt confident that we knew exactly where God was leading. It was obvious that He wanted us to build on the property that we were going to purchase from the federal government's Bureau of Land Management.

One day I received a phone call from my Uncle Lee who had been reading the Las Vegas Review Journal. A major news story had broken stating that the city of Las Vegas had purchased an entire section of the Las Vegas Valley (Section 15). The city was planning to develop a high tech industrial park in the northwest part of the valley, and it had secured every piece of property in Section 15 and was now preparing to take construction bids. The interesting thing about the article was that I knew they didn't have every piece of property in Section 15. The entrance to Section 15 was under contract to Liberty Baptist Church.

Soon after hearing this news, I received a phone call. I was told by the lady on the other end of the line that the Director of BLM wanted to speak with me. "Please hold for Mr. Green," she said. I heard a click. (Please note, Mr. Green's name is fictitious.)

"Reverend Teis?" he asked.

"Yes?"

"This is Joe Green. I'm the Director of Planning and Development for the Bureau of Land Management."

"Oh! Hi, Joe." I replied.

"I need to ask you a question," he continued.

"Well...yes, Mr. Green?" I stammered, my voice belying my calm demeanor.

"Did you get a phone call from Joe McCullugh recently?"

"Yes, sir, I did."

"Did he give you an appraisal for the property that you applied for several months ago?"

"Well, yes, sir, he did," I answered.

"How much was that appraisal for?"

"He told me that he had appraised the property for $180,000 and therefore it would cost us $90,000 if we got it for 50 percent of its fair market value."

"Did he tell you that it is not our normal policy to give appraisals over the phone?" Mr. Green asked.

I thought I detected a note of intimidation in his tone. "Yes, sir, he did," I replied.

"But he did give you an appraisal?"

"Yes, sir."

"Well, Reverend Teis," he began. It sounded like his voice had softened. "Even though it was given to you over the phone, we're going to honor it. But as you might already know, the news broke this morning that the city wants all the property in Section 15. Based on that, the appraisal has soared to $560,000." I felt my breath rush out of my body. "But, since we have already given you the appraisal of $180,000," he continued, "we're going to send you the $90,000 contract. You need to make sure that you sign and get it back to us quickly, because, as I understand it, the city is going to want that piece of property, too."

I breathed a sigh of relief. "Thank you, sir," I replied more calmly. "I really appreciate your forthrightness, and I look forward to receiving that contract."

"Wow!" I thought. "What a phone call! God gave us that piece of property just in the nick of time." Within a couple of days, I got a phone call from the City of Las Vegas. The City Manager's Office wanted me to come in for a private chat. My associate pastor, Bob, went with me to meet with the city manager and his staff.

Harold Foster, the city manager, asked repeatedly if we would be willing to sell the city the property we had purchased from the federal government. I confirmed that we had not yet purchased it, but that we intended to do so. It was the only property we had to build on, I explained. They again asked if we would sell them the property. Feeling a little frustrated, I reiterated that we couldn't sell it because we hadn't yet purchased it. After a brief discussion among themselves, they made an astounding offer.

"We have several twenty-acre parcels available," the city manager remarked. "We would be willing to sell you one of these for the same purchase price you were going to pay for the other parcel, if you'll just release your interest in that property so the city can buy it."

I told him that we would like to help him, but we would have to look at the property first. They told me that they would give us several options. I was a little leery, but I knew God was still in control. The following week we met with Mr. Foster, and he gave us several parcels of land that we could look at in the Las Vegas Valley. After looking at several parcels, we settled on one twenty-two-acre parcel, and I told the city manager we would accept that parcel and I would come up later that week and finalize our agreement.

After telling the city manager that we would accept that parcel, I contacted an older gentleman, a dear friend of our church, who had been in construction in Las Vegas for more years than I had pastored. He was familiar with what would work for construction and what would not. When I took him to the piece of property that I had settled on, he became very upset. He asked me who had advised me to take that piece of property. I told him I thought it was a good location, and I figured one piece of property was as good as another. Mr. Howard was a man of few words, but when he told you something you knew exactly what he meant. He told me in no uncertain terms I had just thrown away the blessing of God. He told me that the property I had accepted would not work for the church. He said he could tell by the lay of the land that it was filled with caliche. Caliche is a hard rock substance that is found underneath the soil in the Las Vegas Valley, and which is almost impossible to dig through. He told me it would cost hundreds of thousands of dollars just to dig through that caliche, and I wouldn't have enough money to build a building. I asked him what I should do. He told me to go back to the city manager and tell him, "I am ignorant concerning property, but there are people who support me and will not support my taking that piece of property. I want you to release me from our agreement." He then told me not to agree to another piece of property until he had walked it first. The Bible says, "in a multitude of counsellors there is safety," so I decided to do exactly what Bill suggested. I went back to the city manager and told him that I was ignorant concerning property and that I would like an opportunity to look at other pieces of property. I was surprised how agreeable the city manager was. I then went out with Bill Howard together, and we found a 22 1/2-acre piece of property that looked perfect. I was later told that it was slated by comprehensive planning to be developed into a city park, but God had other ideas. Over the next several weeks we continued our negotiation with the city of Las Vegas. They drew up a quick claim deed and deeded the property to Liberty Baptist Church. That property had an estimated value of $2 million. We then went to the Bureau of Land Management, a federal agency, and released the property that the city was interested in and they were able to purchase it.

It is very interesting to note that the city of Las Vegas never did use that section for a high-tech industrial park. I believe God allowed us to get the 22 1/2-acre parcel that we finally settled on with a clear deed so that we could sell a portion of it without any government restrictions. Now for the first time in our eleven-year history we finally had a piece of property. Our church went from having nothing financially to having a piece of property worth $2 million.

After much prayer, we decided that we would portion a section of the property and sell it for a housing development. We would use that money to build our church, which we hoped to build debt free. Then I got in touch with Bill Howard who recommended a personal friend of his who was involved in real estate. His name was Kent Midby. Kent was familiar with the buying and selling of commercial real estate. Over the next several months, I had the opportunity of meeting people who were very influential in the valley, and some who were very successful financially. Kent brought many men by to talk about the possibility of purchasing a portion of our property. One man showed considerable interest, and we finally negotiated a buying price for a large portion of the back side of the property. Kent got an appraisal, and they offered us $560,000 contingent on the proper zoning of the property. They put together a site plan and building plans for homes all around the back portion of our property. They submitted the plans to the city, and they were accepted. All the time they were paying us several thousand dollars each month to maintain an open contract with them for the property.

About six months into the negotiations, things began to stall. We had already contacted a contractor and asked them to develop architectural plans for us. I gave them a basic schematic of what I would like to have done, and they put together architectural plans for an octagonal auditorium with an educational wing off the side. When they were finished with the plans, they submitted them to us, and when the plans were finished we were told that the building that we were looking at was going to cost approximately $800,000 to complete. We knew that we only had $560,000 coming from the individual who was trying to purchase our property.

I have never been much of a negotiator, but after eight months of no movement on the sale of our property (knowing he only offered us $560,000, and that we needed $800,000 in order to build our building) I decided to contact the gentleman who was purchasing our property. I told him if he didn't give us our money in the next month that the deal was off. He promptly got back in touch with us, told us that nobody else would want our property, because things were slow, and he was not going to budge. I told him that if we didn't hear from him within a month the deal would be off. At the end of the month he called to extend his contract one more month, and I said no. He was upset, our real estate agent was upset, but we felt confident that God did not want to us to sell to him. I met together with the men of our church and said, "We need $800,000 in order to build what we want to build. So, maybe God doesn't want us to sell the property unless we are going to get $800,000 for it."

After praying together, we decided that instead of selling the property we would put together a plan for modular units on the property, get them approved by the city, move out on our property in modular units, and wait until God gave us somebody who would buy our property for $800,000 so we could build our original building. We started moving in that direction. Our real estate man assured me that nobody was ever going to offer us $800,000 for that piece of property.

The gentleman we were no longer negotiating with came by and said he would give us $600,000, but never $800,000 for that property. We said, "No, thank you."

We moved forward with the modular plan, seeking God's direction. Within the next week the gentleman who offered us $600,000 came in and offered us $650,000. We said, "No, $800,000 is the price."

He accused me of playing hard ball. I had never heard that expression before. I just told him that God did not want us to sell the property unless we got a minimum of $800,000. The next week he came in again and offered us $700,000 and I said, "No."

Our real estate agent, who is a good man, said he could not believe that someone was offering us $700,000 for that piece of property. We knew that God did not want us to sell it for less than $800,000. The following week my real estate agent called and said he could not believe it but someone contacted him and wanted to offer us $800,000 for that piece of property. He wanted to pay us $250,000 down, then at the end of the year pay another $250,000, and then pay the remainder of it. So, in a year and a half we would have all the money, with interest, which would equate to $870,000. I told him we would accept his offer.

The following week the man who we had negotiated with for so long walked in our office and said, "Okay, I will offer you $750,000." I told him we have already sold it for $800,000. He didn't believe me, and later called and said some very unpleasant things to me. God had protected us and allowed us to get $870,000 out of a piece of property that we had purchased for only $90,000. Soon after that, construction began on our property. God miraculously provided so we could build His church. Liberty Baptist Church was a little over thirteen years old when we moved into our first building on February 19, 1991. There had been a number of false starts and stops, but we finally had a base from which we could reach our city.

FROM THEN UNTIL NOW

I believe God graciously allowed Liberty Baptist Church to establish a base of operation so that we could become a mother church in the Las Vegas Valley. In 1991, we also began an effort to get the Gospel to every home in the city. We followed up with a major evangelistic outreach by television and radio. Our growth was slow but steady.

In 1998, we began Liberty Baptist Academy with 43 students. As of this writing we have 160 students enrolled in our school. Our average weekly attendance is 900 people, and we have had a high attendance of over 1,200 people.

As a mother church, we have helped nine other churches begin in Las Vegas and the surrounding area. We've learned much about church planting through trial and error. Since the church's inception, we have committed over $4 million to missions around the world, and have literally seen hundreds of thousands of people trust Christ as their Lord and Saviour. In the following chapters, I will address church planting in more detail and present case studies of our experience.

PART TWO

Practical Tips for Church Planting

SIX

Called to Start a Church

A CHURCH SPONSOR

Upon arriving at Las Vegas in 1977, the first thing I did after moving my wife into our trailer was to go by Gateway Baptist Church to meet with the pastor. I had been a member there before going to Lynchburg to attend college. After he interviewed me, I asked if we could start Liberty Baptist Church as a mission out of Gateway. In doing this, I placed myself under his authority. I had an idea where I wanted to start the church, but he had a different idea. Since I had placed myself under his authority, I took his advice and we moved to the extreme southwest side of town. I thank God that I was under His authority and the authority of the Lord's church. The area I had originally picked soon became a blight on the city.

God will use the authority of the local church to give you direction if you have a submissive spirit. Matthew 16 reveals that God established the church. Again, this is the local church.

First Timothy 3:15 teaches us that the local church is the "pillar and ground of the truth." In the New Testament, churches planted churches and that is the pattern that we are to follow. If God has called you to plant a church in a particular city, I encourage you to look for a pastor in that city who is willing to be your sponsor. This is not always possible, but if it is available, it is the best approach. In some instances, you might have to ask your home pastor to be your sponsor. That would mean that the mission church is starting out of an established church, and you will be accountable to that pastor and that church. Seek your pastor's advice. Nag him! Remember, the squeaky wheel gets the grease! Pastors are very busy. They do not have time to waste. If you have concerns and questions, write them down and speak with him about them. Ask that pastor to write a letter of recommendation that will help you raise support for the new church.

One way to prove yourself to your pastor is to ask if you can teach an adult Sunday school class, and if he would allow you to use that class as a seed to plant a new church. If you do this, you will need to assure him that you will not take any of his existing members without his permission. Pour your life into building that class. Both you and your pastor can get some indication of how successful you will be as a pastor if you can grow that class. If both you and the pastor are confident that you are capable of starting and pastoring a new church, after a year and six months or so, ask the pastor to announce that you are planning to start a new church and that you are going to take some members with you. You need to start as a mission church out of a local church and become an organized church as soon as possible.

RAISING SUPPORT

Often it is necessary for a new church plant to raise support. As you seek to raise support you should create a visual presentation you can show to other preachers. Ask your sponsoring pastor to give you names of pastor friends you can contact. Round up as many names as you can anywhere that you can. Have professionally printed material and a presentation like a missionary going to a foreign field. You are a missionary, you are just going to a field on this side of the globe. Jesus said to go to the uttermost parts of the earth. If you look at where America is located in relation to Israel, you'll see that we are there! Now we need God to provide so that we can obey His command.

Contact pastors and ask them if they would be willing to view your presentation. Get as many pastoral recommendations as you can to share with the pastors that you are going to visit. When you contact them, show them your plan, and explain that you are only asking for support for the first two years. Tell them that you want them to make inverted payments; for example: $100 a month for the first year, and $50 a month the second. Promise them that you will not continue to ask them for money after the second year. I tell men all the time that if they cannot be self-supporting in the United States in two years, then they need to find another place to start a church, or they may be in the wrong business. Again, what you are asking for is full support for the first year, and 50% support the second year. This will cause you to hustle because you know that after twelve months, you are not going to be receiving support, or that it is going to be cut in half. It is amazing how creative we can be and how hard we can work when we have a deadline to meet.

THREE APPROACHES TO CHURCH PLANTING

There are various philosophies of church planting, and as mentioned previously, God has given Liberty Baptist Church the opportunity to be a mother church. Let's take a look at three basic approaches to church planting:

The Many Churches Philosophy

There are church planters who go to a location, establish a church, create an operating organization to run the church, and after three or four years they leave that church, go to another location, and repeat the cycle over and over. After a period of about thirty years, seven to ten Baptist churches will have been planted. Those churches may prosper, or they may fail. This is not an unscriptural approach. In fact, it appears that this was the method the Apostle Paul used in planting churches around the Mediterranean. One of my friends has planted several churches in South America in this fashion, and each church appears to be thriving.

The Mega Church Philosophy

The mega church philosophy is characterized by building one enormous church. The church planter may believe, "God has called me to a particular location, and I plan to stay here the rest of my life. All my efforts will be to enhance this church, grow this church, and develop this church." Neither is this approach unscriptural. Assuming the pastor is not a megalomaniac, when his church begins to run into the thousands, it can be a blessing to other smaller churches. He will also be positioned to reach out to missionaries around the world. If the pastor is a good administrator, he will create many distinct ministries within this one church. Such churches typically have individual, one-on-one discipleship classes; Bible study groups; and a care-giving ministry to minister to individual and family needs.

A mega church can have a major impact on its community and, if well operated, spiritually nourish thousands of people every week. A pastor of a mega church must have the gift of administration. He must be able to impart his vision into the hearts of church leaders so that, as the church grows, the message will not be lost or watered down, neither will church philosophy change. It is imperative that he passes on his doctrinal views, moral standards, and vision to the man who will take his position after his death.

The Mother Church Philosophy

We follow this approach at Liberty Baptist Church. When we came to Las Vegas, it was our dream to develop a mother church. Our philosophy has always been to establish a base of operations from which we could plant or help plant other churches throughout the Las Vegas Valley. When we arrived in 1977, the population was around 400,000. By 2012, it had climbed to around two million. The spiritual need has never been greater. Our desire to develop a teaching church that could win people to Christ, along with a K5–12th grade Christian school where people from fundamental Baptist churches could send their children, has been fulfilled. Moreover, Liberty has helped plant several churches in the valley. Our vision of becoming a mother church has been fulfilled; however, our mission to instruct our members in correct biblical doctrine and to plant new Baptist churches continues.

SEVEN

Developing a Proper Church Concept

"Pastor?" the man queried. "May I ask you a question?"

"Sure." I replied.

"How do you feel when people get upset with you or some aspect of this church and leave? You know, recently, quite a few families have left because they think you are too legalistic."

I pondered the question for a moment. Was this a sincere question, I wondered? Did he desire to know how I really felt or was he indicating that he, too, was preparing to leave? The Bible tells us that there are times that we should answer a fool according to his folly, and there are times we should not.

"Well," I responded, "frankly, I have mixed feelings. Of course I am concerned for those who leave. I believe they are hurting themselves in ways they do not understand. After all, this is not my church, it's God's. And by leaving, they are abandoning a place that the Lord Jesus prepared for them. They, however, do not understand that. As their pastor, I hurt for them, and I want them to get right. On the other hand, when someone develops an unteachable spirit, he or she becomes more of a hindrance to God's work than a blessing. Therefore, I consider such a one's leaving as God protecting His church. When one person chooses to walk away from the will of God and not listen to His Word, I choose to focus on the multitudes who want to receive truth and continue in His church." He made no reply. The expression on his face revealed that he was pondering my answer.

Jesus said, "I will build my church." It is absolutely essential as a church planter that you decide what you believe about the church. Was Jesus talking about a worldwide denomination as many religions teach? Was He speaking about some universal, invisible, intangible church as many believe? Or, was He speaking about an institution that is both visible and local as Baptists have historically taught?

The Apostle Paul wrote his epistles to believers in specific churches in specific cities. He did not address his letters to some ethereal destination. When Jesus called me to establish a New Testament Baptist church, it was not my plan, but His; not my body, but His; not my work, but His. Jesus is the head of every local church. We are just members of that body at a particular location here on Earth. It is absolutely essential that we do it His way and in accordance with His Word. The Bible teaches that God established three institutions:

God Established the Home (Genesis 2:24)

No matter how pop culture describes the family, the Bible-believing Christian knows that the family—the home—consists of one man, married to one woman and, generally, raising children. The home is a single institution that God established in Genesis 2:24. Though it is one institution, it is manifested in individual families all across the globe.

God Established Human Government (Genesis 9)

In Genesis 9, God told Noah after the flood that He would allow men to govern other men. Thus, the institution of human government was established. It is a single institution, but it is manifested in local and higher governments around the globe.

God Established the Church (Matthew 16)

As recorded in Matthew 16:18, Jesus said, "I will build my church; and the gates of hell will not prevail against it." The church is a single institution and yet, as with families and governments, it is manifested locally around the globe. The word "church" is used 117 times in the New Testament. Each time, it is speaking about a local church. In Hebrews 12:23, when the Bible talks about "the general assembly and church of the firstborn," He makes it clear that this is a heavenly assembly. That church will not be a church until it is assembled in Heaven. At the rapture, God will call individual Christians to meet Him in the air, and at that moment, we will be one giant local church.

It is important for a pastor to understand and embrace this concept prior to beginning a New Testament church. A new pastor needs to appreciate the truth, namely, that Jesus established this institution, and it has carried on since the New Testament era. Jesus said that the gates of Hell would not prevail against His church or keep it from moving forward. If you understand that the local church God calls you to establish is His church, you will understand that it is under His authority, and it is not to be run in accordance to your will, but His.

When people get upset with the teaching of His church and leave, or others refuse to join His church, it should not bother the pastor because he understands that they are rejecting the Lord and His authority, not the pastor's. You, as a pastor, will also speak with more authority and, in a real sense, know His power and protection if you understand that it is God's church, not yours.

In Matthew 16:18, Jesus promised to build His church. Jesus watches over His church. The local church has progressed throughout the ages, thus proving the veracity of His words. Jesus commissioned the church in Matthew 28:19–20 and in Acts 1:8. He gave the church its marching orders—to go into all the world as His ambassadors and tell the lost how to be saved. Those who get saved are to be baptized into His local church, and His local church is to teach believers how to live for Him and how to continue reaching others by sharing their testimony with the lost. We could not carry out His commission in our own strength and power. That is why Jesus sent the Holy Spirit, as recorded in Acts 2. The Holy Spirit empowers the church so that we can do what He directs.

We see the church reproducing itself in Acts 13. God tells us in Genesis 1 that each thing He created reproduces after its own kind. Thus, it is only the church that has the authority to send out missionaries to start other local churches. In Acts 13:1–3, holy men of God within the local church at Antioch prayed and fasted and were led by the Holy Spirit to lay hands on Paul and Barnabas and send them into the world to establish other local churches. Throughout the book of Acts, we see a pattern of trained men being sent out from a local church to reproduce that church in other locations. Philip was sent from Jerusalem to Samaria (Acts 8). Philip was also under the authority of the Jerusalem church when he led the Ethiopian eunuch to the Lord (Acts 8:26–40). This likely was the beginning of the church in Ethiopia. Peter was sent from the Jerusalem church to lead Cornelius to the Lord (Acts 10). Saul (Paul) and Barnabas were sent to the Gentiles (Acts 13).

It is essential that we understand that the New Testament church was not some invisible, intangible church. Every time God speaks about His church, there is a reference to something visible and tangible. When a person receives Christ, he is born again, but this time he is born into a new family, the "family of God." When a person is baptized, he is baptized into a local church, just as children are born into specific families.

Every book written by the Apostle Paul recorded in the New Testament, with the exception of Philemon, was written to a local church or to the pastor of a local church. Paul left Timothy and Titus in their respective cities, and he charged them to teach the truth and to see that no other doctrine was taught. They were to set in order things that were lacking and ordain elders in every city. This was Paul's way of telling them to start New Testament churches. In 2 Timothy 2:2, Paul told Timothy to teach others what he had been taught. And what had Paul taught Timothy? How to start and operate a local church.

The book of the Revelation shows how God interacts with local churches. In chapters 2 and 3, we do not see a universal or an all-controlling church. These chapters describe seven independent churches at different locations, all on Earth. Jesus does not tell John to write to the head church and have it relay the message to other churches under it. Jesus walks among the seven candlesticks which are the seven churches, revealing that He is the head of each. Jesus was the head of the church at Philippi, the church at Ephesus, the church at Sardis, and the others. Jesus is the head of each local church, and each local church functions as His body did when He was walking the Earth. His physical body is now in Heaven, seated at the right hand of the Father making intercession for us. It is now our responsibility as His earthly body to tell lost sinners the good news of the Gospel and His kingdom. It is important, also, to understand that if one changes the head, he changes the body. If a man, such as a pope or an archbishop, is the head of a church, it is not God's church. The head of each local church is Jesus.

It is important to understand that when God calls you to begin a local church, you must begin it His way and handle it with care because this is not your church. It is His church. Understanding this concept can give a pastor an awesome sense of accountability, responsibility, and authority that belongs to the local church with Christ as its head. When a pastor has the correct understanding of the biblical concept of the local church, he will be more careful about how he leads and how he feeds the sheep of His pasture.

EIGHT

The Power of Prayer

Going back to that moment I met with Pastor Carter and knew we would be moving to Las Vegas, Anna and I began to discuss what we should do next. We both agreed that it was essential to put together a prayer list. My dear friend and mentor, Dr. C. Sumner Wemp, always says, "If you don't have a prayer list, you won't have a prayer life." I knew that if God wanted us to plant a church, we would need to become earnest about this thing called prayer. After all, it was February, we were graduating in May and the best time of the year to start a church, in my thinking, was in the fall after Labor Day weekend.

In my pastoral theology class, I had the opportunity to hear a Baptist preacher named Peter Lord. Peter had developed a prayer diary he called the 2959, which stood for 29 minutes and 59 seconds with God. I got a copy of it and began using it in my daily devotions. As mentioned, Anna and I created a list of things we would need to start an independent Baptist church in Las Vegas. I wrote down these essential items on a page in my prayer diary that was about prayer for revival in America.

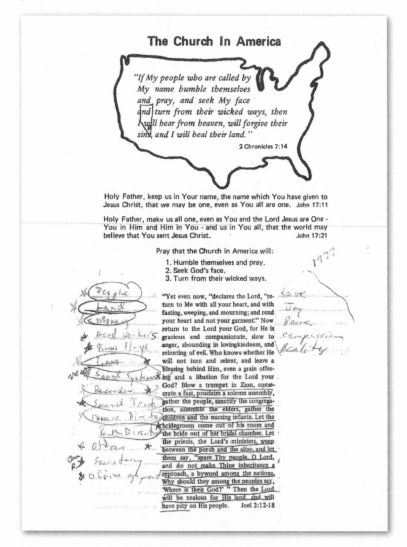

We listed:

1. People

2. A place to meet

3. A love for people

4. Reality in our lives

5. Song books

6. Sound system

7. Chairs

8. A pianist

9. A piano

We needed God's miraculous provision, and we prayed for it daily. John R. Rice once said that any failures he experienced began with prayer failures. Dr. Falwell said that "nothing of eternal value is ever accomplished apart from prayer." If the God of glory, the Lord Jesus Christ has called you to plant a church for Him, then you need to be in constant contact, seeking His direction, leadership and provision. I encourage you to get a prayer diary and write down the things you are praying for. Make prayer a priority in your life.

Years ago, one of my professors named Dan Mitchell told me that I needed to get up every morning at 5 o'clock no matter what else I did. He told me that it was a good time to pray and read my Bible. But, it was important that I get up, just for the sake of getting up. I have found that the only time I really have for personal time with God is in the early morning. Before the day begins, we need to thank Him and ask Him for His daily provision.

If you have not already, set aside a time for daily prayer. Creating a "living" prayer list will help you focus your prayers. It is a living list because you can cross off items as God answers them. Seeing your prayers answered will encourage you to pray even more. Remember, you must establish and maintain a personal walk with the Lord before you can reach lost people with the Gospel.

GET PEOPLE TO PRAY FOR YOU

As we were getting ready to move to Las Vegas, Anna and I asked everybody we knew to pray for us. Today, you can have prayer cards made to distribute for this purpose. People from our church in North Carolina were praying for us every single day. We asked classmates and believers in both of our families to pray for us.

Prayer is a powerful thing. Over the years, when times were lean financially, I would get notes from people who were praying for me. The notes read something like, "Dear Dave, I was praying for you this morning, and God touched my heart to give you this." Often it would be exactly what we needed to get us through the day. I can remember Anna saying to me one day, "David, I need a new pair of shoes." The problem was that we didn't have any money. So Anna and I prayed for God's provision. Before the service that day, my wife prayed specifically that the Lord would provide. When we arrived at the church, a lady walked up to my wife and said, "This morning when I got up, God impressed it on my heart to give you this." She handed my wife an envelope. Inside the envelope was a $100 bill. Anna was excited and asked me what we should do with the $100. I told her she should buy a new pair of shoes. "With the entire $100?" she asked. I told her, "When the Lord gives you money for shoes, you buy shoes!" Knowing my wife, however, she probably bought herself an inexpensive pair of shoes and spent the rest of the money on the kids. The point is, God answers prayer.

FASTING

Along with earnest prayer, let me encourage you to add to your prayer the habit of fasting. Jesus stressed the importance of fasting in addressing certain issues in the spiritual realm.

Fasting is largely a lost practice in Christian circles. Fasting is a discipline in which we say, "Today I am going to give up food for a given period of time so that I can focus on the work that God wants me to do, and ask Him to accomplish some specific task through me or for me." Before fasting, you should check with your doctor to see if you are physically able. There have been times in our ministry when God has called me to fast for two or three days or longer. It is important that you understand how to fast and that you do it correctly.

The first extended fast I went on was for three days. I drank nothing but water. I broke the fast by eating three bowls of chili. Bad idea! When you fast, start off slowly. Fast one meal a day, then the following week, fast two meals in the same day. The following week fast three meals in a day. If you are going to go on an extended fast, longer than three days, make sure you drink something in addition to water and that you ingest something that will keep your digestive system operating. There are some good books on fasting. I suggest you get one and learn how to do it properly. When breaking a fast, you always break it with soft foods such as oatmeal or mashed potatoes (definitely not chili) before ingesting something tougher.

Never neglect the most powerful thing you can do in planting a church—prayer. Make a prayer list and pray daily for the city you are going to and for God's provision of material things and people. Get people to pray for you. Develop prayer cards and distribute them to believers you know. Ask them to call out your name to God. Fast, and when you get hungry, pray and say, "God, I am asking you to meet this special need," and then name it. I would encourage you to read an excellent book on the power of prayer by John R. Rice titled, *Prayer: Asking and Receiving*. He understood the key to powerful prayer.

NINE

Live to Give

I had the privilege of hearing a preacher named Chuck Millhuff who was preaching with Dr. John R. Rice at the Sword of the Lord Conferences during my junior year of college. Chuck preached a message on Luke 6:38 entitled "Giving Living." Luke 6:38 teaches, "Give, and it shall be given unto you; good measure, pressed down, and shaken together, and running over, shall men give into your bosom. For with the same measure that ye mete withal it shall be measured to you again." That is an awesome promise from God. That one verse and message changed my life. The Bible teaches three kinds of giving:

THE TITHE

There are those who teach that the tithe (giving the first 10 percent) is an Old Testament principle, and that anyone who teaches tithing today is a legalist. However, the Bible clearly teaches that the principle of the tithe has always existed.

There was a tithe prior to the giving of the Law. Abraham tithed to Melchizedek, the High Priest of God, as recorded in Genesis 14:20, "And blessed be the most high God, which hath delivered thine enemies into thy hand. And he gave him tithes of all." Jacob promised a tithe to the Lord of all he possessed if God would bless him, as recorded in Genesis 28:22, "And this stone, which I have set for a pillar, shall be God's house: and of all that thou shalt give me I will surely give the tenth unto thee."

There was the tithe under the Law. God promised to bless Israel if they tithed, and to curse them if they did not. God records in Malachi 3:8–10, "Will a man rob God? Yet ye have robbed me. But ye say, Wherein have we robbed thee? In tithes and offerings. Ye are cursed with a curse: for ye have robbed me, even this whole nation. Bring ye all the tithes into the storehouse, that there may be meat in mine house, and prove me now herewith, saith the LORD of hosts, if I will not open you the windows of heaven, and pour you out a blessing, that there shall not be room enough to receive it."

The tithe is in the New Testament. Jesus commended the Pharisees for tithing—one of the few good things He mentioned about them. The principle of the tithe has existed since the beginning of God's Word. I grew up learning from my mother how important it is to tithe, to give back to God the first 10 percent of everything we earn.

FAITH PROMISE GIVING

It wasn't until I was a teenager attending a fundamental Baptist church that I heard of Faith Promise Giving. It was during my senior year of high school that I attended my first Faith Promise service. I learned that, at times, God wants us to ask Him what He would have us to give, trust Him to give us that which we are promising to Him, and then give it back to Him. The biblical example of this is Hannah, Samuel's mother, who prayed that God would give her a son so she could give that son back to Him. First Samuel 1:9–11 records, "So Hannah rose up after they had eaten in Shiloh, and after they had drunk. Now Eli the priest sat upon a seat by a post of the temple of the LORD. And she was in bitterness of soul, and prayed unto the LORD, and wept sore. And she vowed a vow, and said, O LORD of hosts, if thou wilt indeed look on the affliction of thine handmaid, and remember me, and not forget thine handmaid, but wilt give unto thine handmaid a man child, then I will give him unto the LORD all the days of his life, and there shall no razor come upon his head."

Praise the Lord that this past year, Liberty Baptist Church was able to give over $500,000 to missions because of the Faith Promise giving of our members.

GRACE GIVING

Luke 6:38 goes beyond the tithe and faith promise. Grace giving sees a need and is willing to sacrifice to meet it, believing that God will bless and return that gift if the individual is willing to give. Chuck Millhuff, in his message "Giving Living," laid out three principles:

God is our source. God supplies our needs. It is not our clever ability to manipulate circumstances that meets our financial needs. Once I understand that, I will become more dependent on Him.

You must give to get. You must plant to reap. Luke 6:38 teaches, "Give, and it shall be given unto you…." Second Corinthians 9:6 tells us, "But this I say, He which soweth sparingly shall reap also sparingly; and he which soweth bountifully shall reap also bountifully." Many people don't see the blessings of God in their lives because they have never learned to give.

Expect a miracle. It is right for believers to expect God to fulfill His promises.

After Chuck Millhuff preached that message, there was much discussion among the students. However, as a young college student, I decided to follow God's Word. I began to live the principle of giving continually. I have been amazed how God has provided for us over the years. In good economic times and bad, God has always met our needs.

We started Liberty Baptist Church with no promise of support from anyone. Gateway Baptist Church paid the rent on a school building for two months. At the end of those two months, we told them that we no longer needed their support. Our church has been self-supporting and self-propagating since it was two months old without any outside support. There were times when we survived on peanut butter sandwiches, but we always had God's provision. I believe that this was because we learned to tithe, give to missions, and practice grace giving. If you want God's provision in your life, start giving today. Ask God to lead you to someone who has a need, and let God give through you to meet that need. Be faithful in the area of tithing. Get involved in giving to missions, and you will see God's provision in your life.

TEN

Seek Godly Counsel

Proverbs 11:14 says, "Where no counsel is, the people fall; but in the multitude of counsellors there is safety." Proverbs 15:22 teaches, "Without counsel purposes are disappointed: but in the multitude of counsellors they are established." A man who is wise in establishing a church will first get the counsel of godly men, and will throughout his ministry continue to seek their counsel.

Jesus asked, as recorded in Luke 14:28, "For which of you, intending to build a tower, sitteth not down first, and counteth the cost, whether ye have sufficient to finish it?" A wise man counts the cost beforehand. It is a wise man who seeks counsel when he is going to do a work for God. A fool, on the other hand, gets puffed up with pride and thinks he can do it by himself. There are three types of men who will be a help to you if you seek their counsel.

GODLY COUNSELORS

Before I left Bible college, I met with several men who had been involved in church planting and were very well studied in the Word of God. One man, Dr. Ed Dobson, was our Dean of Students. He had planted a church in Buena Vista, Virginia, about 150 miles from the college. Each weekend he would travel there and pastor that church while continuing his duties at the college. I went to him with a list of questions about what I should and should not do in beginning an independent Baptist church. Other men I spoke with included Dr. Woodrow Kroll, who is now the General Director of the Back to the Bible Broadcast; Dr. Dan Mitchell who had been involved in church planting in Texas; and Dr. C. Sumner Wemp. The Bible teaches us in Proverbs 13:20, "He that walketh with wise men shall be wise…." I wanted to talk to these men because I knew they loved the Lord and cared about winning lost people to Jesus Christ. They were men who studied His Word. It is so important to get godly counsel.

OLDER MEN

Seek counsel from older men with business sense and from those who have just "been around" for a long time. Leviticus 19:32 exhorts us, "Thou shalt rise up before the hoary head, and honour the face of the old man…." First Timothy 5:1 warns us, "Rebuke not an elder, but intreat him as a father…." I knew as a twenty-two-year-old man that I did not have the wisdom or insight that comes from age. I had the Word of God, but there is much to be learned from those who have lived long.

I invited my sixth grade teacher to our first service. James Hathaway was an old man from the old school. He allowed no horseplay in his classroom. I got a "swat" from him nearly every day. Over the ensuing years, he became very dear to me. When I came back to Las Vegas, I immediately went to see him and asked if I could come to him for advice from time to time. He was in his early seventies then, some fifty years my senior. He proved to be a valuable source of information over the years.

I became acquainted with Pat Gasaway shortly after beginning Liberty Baptist Church. After leaving the rented school room, we rented a warehouse from him. Pat was an unsaved, crusty old businessman, but he liked me. His office was next door to mine. When I had a business decision to make, I would go to him and ask what he would do. One time he replied, "Well, preacher, I know what I would do. But you can't do that because it's unethical." Years later, Pat got saved, and today he is in Heaven.

I was thirty years old when I met seventy-seven-year-old H.G. McDaniels. He was a great source of inspiration and knowledge when it came to business. About the same time, I met a man named Bill Howard. Bill was an entrepreneur. He was a very wealthy Pentecostal businessman. He and his wife Dottie loved Anna and me and the rest of our family. He attended our church only two or three times, but any time I was making a major business decision I would go to Bill for advice. His counsel probably saved us hundreds of thousands of dollars when we were about to acquire our property from the city. Older men are a great resource for a young church planter. I do not recommend that you appoint them to any official church board, but just keep their phone numbers handy and let them know that you value their opinions. God established you as the pastor of the church. Therefore, you need to make the decisions, but it is wise to get the input of older men.

INFORMED COUNSELORS

Interview men who have done it right. Ask them questions. Ask for step-by-step instructions, then do what you're told. There are few things more frustrating than having someone come to me, ask me what I would do in that situation, and then ignore my advice. When listening to advice, you need to eat the fish and spit out the bones. If you're going to take someone's time who is experienced in church planting and ask for advice, at least give him the courtesy of following some of it. This book is not the final word on church planting. However, it contains the insights of a man who has spent many years getting insights from others who have done it.

ELEVEN

Do It Now

Over the last thirty-five years, I have had many young men come and tell me that they were planning to start a particular type of ministry. I have always asked the same thing, "What are you doing now?" I get answers like:

"Well, right now I'm going to school...."

"Well, right now I'm working full time...."

"Oh, I can't possibly do any of this now. Right now I'm involved in...."

Moving to another city is not going to change who you are. It is important if you plan to do something in another city, that you start doing that "something" now. If you plan to knock on doors when you move to the city where God has called you, start doorknocking now! Practice now. If you plan to distribute tracts, do it today. You should promote your local church now. If you are planning on pastoral teaching, then you need to get involved in a teaching ministry now.

Learn how to communicate effectively. Get together with friends who will critique the way you preach. I encourage you to practice your sermon delivery method and record it. If you fall asleep while listening to yourself, then understand that you may be tormenting other people if you ask them to come to church and listen to you. Imitate the good delivery techniques you see in other preachers. There is nothing wrong with improving your style by listening to good preachers. In college classes all across the country, people are learning how to sing by listening to other people sing. You learned how to talk by listening to other people talk. It is amazing how the voice of a young lady will sound so much like that of her mother, even if the tonal quality is different. The inflections and other characteristics of her voice will remind you of her mother. The same is true of sons and their fathers. They are not inherited traits, but learned.

We learn by imitation. It is sad that the devil has put it in the hearts of young preachers that, though they may admire a particular preacher or a particular preaching style, they shouldn't imitate it, that it's "unspiritual." The Apostle Paul said, "Be ye followers of me, even as I also am of Christ" (1 Corinthians 11:1). If you hear a preacher that you think is particularly good, listen to him. Ask yourself, "What makes me want to listen to him?" Is it only the content of the message? Is it his delivery? Is it his repetition of various points? Is there excitement in what he is saying? How does he draw the crowd into his message? Learn to preach by listening to others. And then learn to listen to people who critique you. A pastor said to me, "I am doorknocking every single day, and I am seeing people get saved. I am also seeing them come to church, but they don't come back."

There are a few reasons why people that come to church don't stay:

1. They disagree with your message. If your message is Bible-based, and that offends them, that is not your problem. Let them leave.

2. They may not feel welcome. Remember, we're Baptists, not Presbyterians! It's okay, even recommended, to show genuine love even to strangers coming through the front doors for the first time. A newcomer will be able to quickly determine if this is a warm, living body of worshippers, or the cold corpse of a body in need of resurrection. It has been said repeatedly, "People don't care how much you know until they know how much you care." It is important that you have a warm and friendly church.

3. The preaching is bad. Another reason people do not come back is because the preaching is bad. You really need to listen to yourself preach. Like it or not, we are in the twenty-first century. People are educated. People are not

motivated by guilt. People will respond to an intelligent presentation of a Bible-based message that will help them. (See more about why churches fail in Appendix C.)

If you plan on preaching and teaching, do it now and work to perfect it. If you plan on following up, do it now. Discipleship is a very important part of any ministry. There are Christians all around you that need to grow in Christ. Start developing a discipleship ministry now. If you don't serve now, you probably won't serve later. If you plan on doorknocking, do it now; if you plan on giving out tracts, do it now; if you plan on preaching and teaching, do it now; and if you plan on discipling, do it now.

TWELVE

A Step-by-Step Approach

Once you have placed yourself under the authority of a sponsoring mother church, local or otherwise, it is important that you begin implementing your plan.

STEP 1. SECURING A LOCATION

By this time, you and your sponsoring pastor will have identified an area of the city where you want to plant the new church. The next step is to identify a particular location. If someone in your sponsoring church is a real estate agent, ask if he knows of any suitable commercial properties for lease. In addition, you may want to consider some of the following:

Private schools. Usually these buildings are empty on weekends and make an excellent place to begin. The negative with renting space from a multi-use facility like a school is that you have to move in and move out weekly. You can't move in until Saturday night and you have to move out after the Sunday evening service.

Pre-schools. Often pre-schools have a large gathering area that can serve as an auditorium.

Funeral homes. Very few funeral services take place on Sunday morning; therefore, their chapels which are often very ornate are an excellent place to have a worship service. When one church here in Las Vegas was able to start in a funeral home, it gave them a very beautiful auditorium to use every Sunday morning. They were also able to use the facilities on Sunday night and Wednesday night, and they did so for two years.

Centrally-located warehouses. An unused warehouse can be an excellent place to start because you can modify the interior to suit your purposes. Also, you can hold midweek services without having to move in one afternoon and out that evening.

Storefronts. Storefronts, particularly if located in a strip or mini-mall, are excellent. Normally the stores don't open early on Sunday morning, there is plenty of parking space, and the nature of the place draws the public, some of whom may be considering finding or joining a church.

Public schools. Elementary, junior high, and high schools have assembly areas that make them an excellent place to start a church. Again, the downside is moving in on Saturday evening and out on Sunday night.

Ranch-style homes. If you can get a ranch style home on an acre of property, that would provide you with parking and, if you are able to remodel the living room, you can sometimes get seating for 60–80 people.

Don't be anxious. Remember, if God has called you to plant a church, He will provide a place. Accessibility and visibility are important for a new church. Keep these in mind while you're looking. We found that our most challenging years for growth were when we were in a warehouse building in an industrial area of the city. Some don't feel comfortable attending church in an industrial area. You must remind them that they are the church, not the building. Also remember that people will go out of the way for a good product. Cracker Barrel Restaurants are sometimes located in very inconvenient spots to reach, however, because of their reputation people are willing to drive out of their way to their locations because of the quality of their product.

STEP 2. APPLY FOR A USE PERMIT

Once you've found a location, you will need to apply to the County or City Government for a Use Permit. Most cities are lenient when it comes to churches. Churches can normally meet in any zone; you just have to get permission. You will need to stop at your city offices and complete the paperwork. Before signing a contract for a lease, make sure you have a contingency that voids the contract if you cannot acquire a use permit.

STEP 3. FLYERS AND TRACTS

Develop an attractive color flyer. It is a good idea to go first class since most people will evaluate what your church might be like from the appearance of your flyer. There are several independent Baptist churches that have the necessary equipment and can personalize your flyer for you.

Your first 10,000 flyers should include:

- A personal invitation from you
- A statement describing the church, (e.g., nursery, Sunday school classes, solid Bible teaching, traditional hymns, etc.)
- You will want it to include a picture of you and your wife, and, if applicable, your children.
- The times and dates of each service and a special announcement about your opening day, along with your church address and a map to your location.
- Your website address should be prominent. The internet today is what the yellow pages were thirty years ago (more will be said about the internet in Step 11).
- Include the plan of salvation. Make sure when you give the plan of salvation it is done in such a way that they understand the full Gospel message (See Appendix A).

STEP 4. DOOR KNOCKING

Shortly before we left Lynchburg, Virginia, Dr. Jerry Falwell stood in the pulpit one day and made a fist. He raised his knuckles in the air and said, "Boys, I want you to know that these knuckles have knocked on every single door in Lynchburg." If you would like to know the secret of building a church, that is it. It is plain hard work. Dr. Paul Chappell knocked on 500 doors per week for the first 18 months straight. That is why his church was running 3,000 people after only 15 years and now consistently runs over 4,500 on any given Sunday with over 8,000 people in membership. This is where the rubber meets the road. This is where success or failure will be determined. This is where the going gets tough and, if you're equally tough, you'll get going! You may knock on several hundred doors before someone shows an interest in what you have to say.

When Anna and I came to Las Vegas, it was 110 degrees. We knew we only had eight weeks before our church was to start. We went door to door every afternoon. Set a goal to knock on no less than one hundred doors per day. If you aim at nothing, you will hit it every time. The more doors you knock on, the more likely it is that you will find someone to come to church the next Sunday. Remember, your goal in going door to door is not necessarily to lead someone to Christ in the initial visit. It is to invite them to a new church that is starting, and get the Gospel into their hands and hearts. Your goal is to let them know about the church, and, if they show an interest, to get their names and addresses so you can contact them later and remind them about the services. If you have an opportunity to share the Gospel, then of course you need to follow the leading of the Holy Spirit, but the main purpose is getting people to church.

STEP 5. TWELVE-WEEK RECRUITS

Recruit as many volunteer doorknockers as you can for twelve weeks before the first service. Ask your pastor if you can announce in his church that the people are welcome to help you with your twelve-week doorknocking campaign. Contact your alma mater and ask if you can get a singing group or an evangelistic team from your college to come and help you plant this church. If you can't, get one from another Christian college that is willing. In helping start Southern Hills Baptist Church in the southwest part of the valley, we got teams from Pensacola Christian College, West Coast Baptist College, and several others. Often, youth groups from local churches will take you on as a mission's trip. This is a great help in planting a new church. The more soulwinners you can get to help you go door to door, the better. If you recruit a team, make sure you have things ready for them when they arrive. You will be responsible for feeding them, possibly lodging them, and having packets of tracts ready for them to hand out. We keep our tracts in stacks of fifty so that we can keep count of how many doors we have knocked.

STEP 6. FOLLOW UP STEPS

Follow up on prospects from the doorknocking campaign. Make sure that if one of your helpers meets someone at the door, that you follow up with a personal visit. That is what your evenings are for. Tuesday evenings, you and your wife should be visiting. Wednesday evenings, you should be in church; Thursday evenings, you and your wife should be visiting; Friday evenings, you and your wife should be visiting; Saturday, all day, you and your wife should be revisiting the people you contacted throughout the week. These follow-up visits are essential and, generally, pay handsome dividends. Some specific steps are provided below:

1. Show people you love them and care about them.

2. Carry an 8.5 x 11 inch sheet of paper in your pocket. Fold it in half three times creating eight folds, it will be the size of one of your tracts. If you fold it correctly, you will have a place for sixteen prospects on one 8.5 x 11 sheet of paper. You carry that behind your tracts in your pocket. Whenever you find people who have the slightest bit of interest in your church plant, get their names, addresses, telephone numbers, and email addresses. If they have children, get their names and ages. It is wise to follow up with a phone call each week and an occasional note in the weeks leading up to Opening Day.

3. Send a reminder letter each week.

The last week before your first service, revisit all your prospects. When visiting, visit in new neighborhoods near your church first. People that are living in new neighborhoods are often looking for a new place to worship. Lord willing, yours will be that church. By the time opening day comes, they will have had a phone call, a letter, and a personal visit the week before.

STEP 7. MAP OUT AREAS OF INTEREST

Map out areas that you are going to doorknock, and map other areas that you are going to mail to, such as gated communities and apartment complexes. Get the maps to the doorknockers.

STEP 8. MAIL OUT

Mail out as many invitations to homes in the surrounding area as you can. If you are in a smaller town, try to recruit churches to help you pay for a letter to be mailed to every single home in the city inviting them to your opening service. When we helped start Southern Hills Baptist Church, we knocked on 35,000 doors and mailed the same information to another 35,000 homes. On opening Sunday, there were 265 people in the service.

STEP 9. CHECK OUT ADVERTISING COSTS

See what advertising you can get. Some localities have community newspapers that provide free advertising. Newspapers often have free PSAs (Public Service Announcements). Check out the announcements on the local Christian radio station. Contact Bearing Precious Seed, and see what it would cost for you to use the Gospel of John & Romans going door to door. You might consider having a TV ad following a conservative preaching program in your city, if you can find one.

After opening Sunday, write a letter to all the prospects regarding the great success, no matter how many people you had in services. It was a great success because the church has started. Write with a positive, upbeat spirit. After the Opening Service, write a letter to all who attended the first service. Thank them for coming, and invite them to come again.

STEP 10. ROAD SIGNS

Several weeks before the first service, post temporary road signs along the main thoroughfare so people will be aware of your new presence. Include your web address on the road signs.

STEP 11. THE INTERNET

By far, one of the most valuable and inexpensive tools for advertising your church today is the internet. There are various ways that you can use the internet. First, have someone design a sharp website. This should be completed before your twelve weeks of doorknocking begins. Each week your website should be updated, reminding people of the special service days that are coming. Everything you print, every sign you post, every advertisement that you place should have your website address in a prominent location.

Your website should include the following:

- A personal note from you
- A picture of you and your family
- If possible, a video of you introducing your family and the new church
- A map to the church with clear directions
- The dates and times of services
- The address of the church
- A tab where the Gospel is given

There are several fundamental Baptist churches who will be willing to help you design your website. Make sure that your website is designed well. This could possibly be the first introduction that someone has to your church. Make sure it is an able ambassador.

STEP 12. THE FIRST SUNDAY SERVICE

All programs should be ready and in place for the first service (i.e., Sunday school, morning worship, Sunday evening as well as Wednesday evening). Let the people see this church as one that is already operating. The Gospel should be given clearly. The hymnal music should be as lively as possible. Sunday School lessons should be based on solid Bible teaching. Begin discipleship early. Conduct yourself like a pastor, dress like a pastor, and act like a pastor.

STEP 13. A WEEK OF MEETINGS

The first week of a new church should begin with a series of meetings: Sunday evening through Wednesday evening. At each of these meetings, a nursery should be provided as well as classes for children ages two to eleven. An exciting special speaker should be invited to preach; a speaker who understands the purpose and operation of a New Testament Baptist church. Each night should have exciting music and a message dealing specifically with the birth, care and feeding of a New Testament Baptist church. Below are some suggested topics for the week:

- "Why God Began the Local Church"—The purpose of the church
- "You and Your Church"—How you fit and relate to the church
- "What Is a Real Church"—What we believe and why
- "The Responsibility of the Church"—The Great Commission/Soulwinning & Discipleship

This week of meetings is designed to energize your base and excite people about this new church. One final suggestion would be to try to get a Baptist college ensemble or a singing team from the mother church to help provide the special music for each night during the first week.

THIRTEEN

Becoming an Effective Preacher

She wasn't a very big woman. Neither was she particularly attractive. But she walked into a classroom filled with young, inattentive college students and immediately got their attention. How? She moved to the front of the class, stood behind the podium, and with the vigor of a twenty-year-old soccer player, kicked a small, tin garbage can across the classroom. The loud clang caught everyone's attention. "Do you know what I've just done?" she asked confidently. Her eyes looked from one student to the next as though she expected an answer. "I've just gotten your attention! And if you want to be an effective communicator, you've got to learn to 'kick the can.'" The sad thing is, today, many preachers don't know how to "kick the can." You may have the most important message in the world—and if you're a Gospel preacher, you do—but if you don't learn to speak effectively, your message will go unheard and unheeded. The one thing that will draw people back to a church plant is the effectiveness of the pastor and the power behind his message. The "Be Attitudes" of an effective preacher are discussed in this chapter.

BE A RELEVANT PREACHER

It is essential to understand your audience and your culture. It is ineffective to stand before a group of twelve-year-old boys and talk to them about how to be an effective witness at the office; or to stand before a group of ladies and talk to them about the responsibilities of a godly husband. Rather, they need to learn how to be godly, submissive wives. A preacher must know his audience. The Word of God is relevant to every age; however, the way it is presented makes it age specific. When pastoring a new church, you must begin with the presupposition that no one understands the Gospel or your religious lingo. Your very first Sunday, you should be sure to present a clear, concise Gospel message, and from that point forward, you should make sure, as you teach, that you do not assume that anyone has any preconceived notions about what your church stands for. You must understand that many of them do not understand any of the issues that may be important to you. If a more mature believer approaches you about the simplicity of your message, or asks why you explain things in detail, let him know that you are very thankful that God sent him as a mature believer to your church. Explain that you are preaching with such detail because you are concerned that every new believer and every visitor also have a clear understanding of the Gospel message and the Scriptures. Implore his help in reaching and explaining things to new believers. Anna and I were trained in fundamentalism. I was shocked as I went from door to door that people did not know what an independent, fundamental Baptist church was. They did not know the names of my spiritual heroes. They were totally unaware of my background and what I was trying to do. It was my job to know their culture, their background, and how I could best relate to them and bring them to the truth of the Gospel. We do not need to compromise with our culture, but we do need to understand where people are coming from so we can help them live a Christian lifestyle in the culture of their day. You need to understand your audience and your culture so you can preach messages that will reach your target audience and help believers be an effective light in the culture in which they live.

BE A PASSIONATE PREACHER

There are few things worse than walking into a Baptist church and hearing a man rattle off the dynamic life-changing truths of the Gospel with the enthusiasm of a window clerk from the Department of Motor Vehicles: "NEXT." John Wesley said, "Catch on fire with enthusiasm and people will come from miles around to watch you burn."

If your message is not exciting enough to you to reveal your passion in the pulpit, then please do not start an independent Baptist church. If it's only form and religion or addressing facts, if you have no passion for lost souls that shows, then planting a church is not for you. The greatest news in the world is that Jesus Christ, God in human flesh, became a man and suffered and died to pay the penalty for our sins, that He rose again three days later, having paid for our sins. The Gospel is the power of God unto salvation to everyone that believes. It should never be presented in a "hum-drum" manner. We live in a world that is filled with sin, a culture that is in the midst of demise. As I am writing this book, America is being led down a path of socialism by social progressives. Our country is sponsoring abortions not only in this country, but also around the world. Our president has denied that we are a nation that was founded on biblical principles. The president declared June as national Gay and Lesbian month. Teachers in public schools are teaching our children that they are just another form of animal life. Any mention of God is being stripped from our public institutions; our financial institutions are crumbling; unemployment is surpassing 10 percent; and many are facing bankruptcy. These are the challenges that the people listening to you preach are facing every day. In the twenty-first century, people need to know that there is a God who cares about and loves them and is passionately interested in their unique problems. You need to stay relevant, passionate, and exciting in your presentation if you are going to help people through these uncertain times.

BE A DOCTRINAL PREACHER

Make sure that in every message you stress the importance of doctrine. As you are studying for a particular Sunday morning message, ask yourself, "What Bible doctrine is being presented as I prepare this message?" It might be the deity of Jesus Christ; His virgin birth; the inerrancy of Scripture; or the doctrine of sin and the fall of man. Whatever your message, it should be based on sound biblical doctrine. We live in an age when pastors of some mega churches, as well as smaller ones, are de-emphasizing doctrine. In fact, there are some who boast that their major doctrine is that they have none! I have heard some independent Baptist preachers mock liberals and neo-evangelicals for not teaching doctrine while they fail to teach it themselves. Your message should not just be relevant, it should not just be passionate, it should be one that is filled with correct biblical doctrine.

BE A WELL-STUDIED PREACHER

About a year after we started our church, someone gave me a series of tapes by a preacher who mentioned that he spent thirty-five hours a week studying the Word of God. I was struck in my heart. That wasn't true in my case, I knew. You will probably find it's not going to be the case for you, either.

As a church planter, you are going to be visiting people, looking for buildings, organizing, doorknocking, and doing follow-up visits. Doing all of that is not going to give you the time to study that a pastor in an established church would have. Nevertheless, it is essential that you be a well-studied preacher. You need to schedule in your week a time to study. Let me suggest that you do a message series on Sunday morning and preaching through books of the Bible on Sunday and Wednesday evenings. This will save you time in message preparation. You will not have to identify a new topic to preach on each week. You can preach on the next point in your series on Sunday morning and in the next few verses from your Bible on Sunday and Wednesday evenings. It will also help your people become systematic in their Bible reading and spiritual growth. It is important that you do not just stand up and spout off on current events you know nothing about! If you are going to make dogmatic statements from the pulpit, make sure you can back them up with Scripture and documented material. Make sure you preach your convictions and not your preferences. Years ago, I heard Dr. Robert Knutson, a pastor in Southern California, say, "Most Baptist preachers preach their preferences as if they were convictions and drive away any thinking man from their church." When you preach, preach Bible convictions that you have studied and that you can fully defend from the Word of God. Be a well-studied preacher.

BE A PRACTICAL PREACHER

Tell people how to apply your message to their lives. Tell them what God wants them to do with the message. Tell your audience how to have the right kind of family and the right kind of friends. Teach them how to have the right relationships on the job and with their neighbors. Teach them how to be good citizens. Teach them how to communicate the Gospel to their lost friends. Be practical in your preaching so people can apply your teaching to their lives.

BE AN UNDERSTANDABLE AND SYSTEMATIC PREACHER

Years ago, Dr. C. Sumner Wemp gave us the simple acrostic KISS—Keep It Simple, Stupid. You do not have to impress people with your intellect. They are not there to find out how great an intellectual you are. You do not have to impress them with the fact that you have learned a new word each week from your online educational program. What you need to do is take the Word of God and make it as understandable as possible so that all in the service can benefit from your message. One way to achieve this is to prepare a systematic outline for your message. Read your homiletics books on outlining. Many preachers joke about the three points and a poem method of teaching. However, that simple formula helps get the truth across in a very powerful way. You don't have to limit your message to three simple points. However many you have, delineate them clearly so your listeners can follow your outline as you present God's Word. Be an understandable and systematic preacher.

BE A PRACTICING PREACHER

A preacher needs to practice what he preaches. Woe unto that pharisaical hypocrite who stands before his people and tells them to read their Bible every day, but does not follow what he teaches; who tells his people to pray every day, but seldom prays himself; who tells his listeners that they ought to be soulwinners, but seldom knocks on a door himself; or who tells his people that they ought to be passing out tracts, but seldom does so himself. Woe to the pastor who teaches the love of Jesus Christ but is so self-centered that he seldom expresses his love toward others because he is too "busy." Woe to the pastor who preaches on the family, but ignores his own. Woe to the preacher who teaches that husbands are to love their wives, but fails to show his love for his wife to the extent that she feels unloved and neglected. Preacher, your wife is your primary responsibility. She needs to look better than you, dress better than you, and be treated better than you. Do not stand up on Sunday morning in your "holy robes" with your great oratory skills to impress the crowd unless you are practicing what you preach. Be a practicing preacher.

BE A BIBLE PREACHER

Do not just open the Bible, read a verse, and then tell one story and then another. Use the Bible as your base. Expository Bible preaching should be the norm for independent Baptist preachers. There is nothing wrong with a textual or topical message. We need to preach from time to time on topics that are facing our people. However, a topical message should be based firmly in the Word of God. There are many things today taught in independent Baptist churches that are not found in Scripture. If you are going to preach a topical message, make sure it is a Biblical topic. Whether you preach an expository, textual, or topical message, as an independent Baptist preacher standing for the King James Bible, be sure that you are preaching Bible messages and that you are a Bible preacher.

BE A GOSPEL PREACHER

An independent Baptist preacher should be a Gospel preacher. In every message you preach, whether it is Old or New Testament, you should include the Gospel. Often a preacher can find a way to insert the Gospel into his message. However, if that is not the case, stop somewhere in your message and tell people that Jesus Christ, God in human flesh, suffered and died to pay the penalty of our sins according to the Scriptures. He was buried, and three days later, according to the Scriptures He rose from the dead having paid for our sin debt in full. He was seen by hundreds of people, and He went back to Heaven. Since He has paid our sin debt, we can know we are going to Heaven if we call upon Him and ask Him to be our Lord, our Saviour, and our God. Be a Gospel preacher. Don't just tell people they need to get saved. You need to tell them how to get saved and explain to them the provision that was made for them to be saved. A Baptist preacher should be a Gospel preacher. You can be an effective preacher of the Gospel if you have the passion; if you deliver the message; and if you'll keep it practical, relevant, and simple. Appendix B gives a clear Gospel presentation.

FOURTEEN

Living by Principles and Priorities

After thirty-five years of watching many people plant churches, I've seen many dedicated men lose their families because they put their churches before their families. Our church has not grown as fast as some others, but Anna and I determined before we came to Las Vegas that we were going to live by biblical principles and priorities and not allow our family to suffer in order to build a work. Your family ministry will either validate or invalidate your church ministry.

COMMIT TO GUARD YOUR TIME

Colossians 4:5, "Walk in wisdom toward them that are without, redeeming the time." Your time and your priorities are very important.

Guard your time with God.

Ephesians 5:18 says, "And be not drunk with wine, where in is excess; but be filled with the Spirit." Galatians 5:16 says, "This I say then, Walk in the Spirit, and ye shall not fulfil the lust of the flesh."

You must have time alone with God. You must guard that time every single day. You need to have a time of prayer, a time of Bible reading, and a time when you are refreshed in the Word of God and you are loving Him.

Guard your time with your wife.

Ephesians 5:25 says, "Husbands, love your wives, even as Christ also loved the church, and gave himself for it." First Timothy 3:2 says that one of the qualifications for a bishop is that he must be "blameless, the husband of one wife...."

You must have time set aside for your wife. When we got married, Anna and I determined that we were going to take every Monday off. We also determined that we were going to take at least a two-week vacation every year. This is not a time to do anything with anyone else. It is time for us to minister to one another. Ministry is twenty-four hours a day, seven days a week, but you must take time to minister to one another also.

People ask me if I stop pastoring on Monday. I reply, "No. I pastor my family on Mondays. That is the day I take to minister to their needs." That might include watching TV with them or playing games. It might be going to the park or taking a trip to Disneyland, but they need a pastor just like everyone else. I've heard preachers actually brag about not taking family vacations. How foolish. God created the institution of the family first. The church is to build the family of God, but God does not expect you to build His family at the expense of your own.

Guard your time with your children.

Proverbs 22:6 says, "Train up a child in the way he should go: and when he is old, he will not depart from it." You need to make your life and ministry family centered. Our children ministered with us in everything we did. We played together, we worked together, we went on vacations together, and we went to preaching conferences together. We would not allow anything to take us away from spending time with our children. In our marriage, Anna was number one to me, I was number one to her and our children were number one to us. Your church ministry comes after your family ministry.

Guard your time with your ministry.

Tuesday night, be out on visitation. Wednesday night, be in church. Thursday night, have discipleship. Friday night, work with youth. Saturday, be out on visitation and soulwinning.

The year we started Liberty Baptist Church, a dear friend of mine, Lewis, started a church in North Carolina. He was married while we were going through school and had two precious children and a lovely wife. He became very aggressive in his church building. We kept in contact from time to time, though we were on opposite sides of the country. When our church was two years old, we were averaging a little over 150 people. We were in a rented facility and were nowhere near purchasing a piece of property. On our vacation that year, we traveled back to North Carolina. I visited my friend. He was living in a beautiful home that made my house look like a shack. His church was running close to 500 people, and they were getting ready to break ground on a new building. He showed me around, and while we were talking he asked, "Teis, you know the difference between you and me and why you'll never build a large church?"

"What's that?" I replied.

"You play, and I don't!" Lewis continued, "You're running 150 now and I'm running 500, yet you're taking a vacation!"

"I guess you're right, Lewis," I responded. "But I really feel my family needs to come first." He told me that he had not taken a day off in two years and "…that's why God is blessing my ministry."

Lewis was a dynamic speaker, had a wonderful personality, and he worked very hard. All are great qualities if controlled by the Holy Spirit. However, he neglected his wife and children. He built a beautiful building, but three years later he was out of the ministry. His wife got tired of playing second fiddle to his ministry. His children resented not having a father. The last I heard, Lewis was a womanizing drunk and out of the ministry—his lovely family destroyed. This story has been repeated over and over. Don't allow this to happen to you. Commit to guard your time and make your family your FIRST priority.

DON'T LET YOUR WIFE WORK OUTSIDE OF THE CHURCH

As the man of the house, your job is to support your family. First Timothy 5:8 tells men that if they don't provide for their families, they are worse than infidels. As a church-planting pastor, your wife needs to be with you. I could tell you story after story of men in the ministry who have had affairs, many with their secretaries or some other woman in the church. Whether you think it's true or not, your wife needs to be with you. She needs to be with you more than you need to have great food, fancy clothes, a nice car, or a new house. Your wife needs to be with you more than she needs to be with her own children. Your wife needs to be involved intimately in your ministry! She does not need to financially support you. What she needs is to be your HELP MEET! I have offered this advice to many men and have been mocked for it. It is a bad example for your wife to work outside your ministry. It will divide her time and not allow her to be the pastor's wife that God wants her to be. People ask, "Well then, how do you survive?"

LIVE CHEAP AND LEARN HOW TO PRAY

God will supply your needs if you do it His way. You may not have a whole lot, but you will have everything you need. As a church planter, you need to determine to plant your roots deep. You need to determine to endure hardship without giving up. You need to stay where God leads you until the work is done and He calls you somewhere else. You need to pray hard; preach hard; work hard; and, when you play, play hard! Your wife should have the same philosophy—this is a JOINT effort! Your wife needs to work hard with you! She should be by your side continually. Her energies should be spent by your side, helping you develop your God-given ministry. It is not good if she is at home nesting, and not working with you. Her work is to help you build the family and the ministry.

FIFTEEN

Successes and Failures in Church Planting

Having helped nine other churches begin here in the Las Vegas and surrounding areas, we've learned a few things from our experiences. Some were reinforcing, and others, not so much.

Within six months of establishing Liberty Baptist Church in 1977, a fellow college graduate moved to Las Vegas. At that time our church was located on the extreme southwest end. He told me that he wanted to begin an independent Baptist church on the extreme southeast side. It sounded like a great idea. Since we were self-supporting, and I had come to Las Vegas with the dream of establishing a mother church, we told him we would do anything we could to help. However, our funds were very limited, and so, much of what we did was in the area of prayer and encouragement.

After about six months, the pastor closed the doors and brought his members across town to Liberty Baptist Church.

Maybe you can already see some of the mistakes we made:

1. When a church is young and has not established itself (does not have a solid base of operation because it is still in a rented facility), it should not reach out to others so confidently and begin to act like a mother church. There may be some rare exceptions in which God will bless, but generally and as already mentioned, the Lord grows His people and His church day by day. Long-term goals are achieved over time, not overnight. Remember in the beginning, your church may not be mature enough to help another start.

2. A mature church is a self-supporting one that has a permanent home. At only six months, we were still in a rented facility and not ready to help another church begin. I wanted to be an encouragement, but we should not have tried to establish another church while we were still in our infancy.

A few years later, in 1980, a member of our church approached me about helping him start a church in Henderson, Nevada, about twenty miles southeast of Las Vegas. The man was not only a member, he was also a dear friend who I believed had a heart for lost souls. He did not graduate from a Bible college or a Bible institute; nevertheless, we determined that we should help him. We assisted in finding a place for the new church to meet and provided financial support at $1,000 a month. What I hadn't realized was that we still weren't ready to help start another church. The need was evident, but a need does not always indicate a call. A good man can have a passion to accomplish something, but if he doesn't have the proper training and he doesn't have his family's unified support, he is setting himself up for failure.

The good news is that his church began to grow. However, over a relatively short time, this young man began to get more and more caught up in Calvinistic doctrine. I and other supporters spoke with him about the importance of correct biblical doctrine. We finally had to withdraw our spiritual and financial support when it became apparent that he was teaching error and refused to change.

He closed his church after a few years. God will not bless false teaching no matter how sincere pastors are. Sincere pastors teaching doctrinal error are sincerely wrong!

There are three important lessons I learned from this experience:

1. Not everyone who feels that he is called by God to start a church is able.
2. If one doesn't have the determination to complete Bible studies at a recognized college, he may not have the steadfastness to stick it out when times get tough in his church.

3. A man planting a Baptist church needs to be secure in his doctrinal beliefs, secure in his practice of Bible truths, and secure in his family's support.

In 1999, another young man came to the Las Vegas Valley. He came from a solid, Bible-believing Baptist church. He had earned a degree from a well respected Bible college and had been on staff at a respected church for several years. He told me that he felt God had called him to the southeast part of Las Vegas to begin an independent Baptist church. He asked for our assistance. After confirming his credentials and references, I spoke with him and his wife. Subsequently, I spoke with the men of our church and we decided to help him. We identified a young couple in our church, along with a single college-age student who lived in that area and agreed to assist the young pastor and his wife by helping them with the Sunday school and nursery.

We drove them around the southeast section of Vegas to help them find a meeting place. After looking at several possibilities, they selected a school building which reminded me of how Liberty Baptist Church had started. We helped with the production costs of tracts and supported him for the first three months at $2,000 a month. Following that, we supported his new church at $200 a month for two years. I praise God that, as of the time of this writing, they are about to celebrate their twelfth anniversary. They also plan to move into permanent facilities in the near future. I believe that their efforts will continue to blossom into a tremendous work here in the valley.

In 2002, we had the privilege of helping three more men of God who felt called to the Las Vegas area to plant churches. The first felt called to start in the extreme northwest section. The second believed that God was calling him to the southwest side of town. The third felt led of God to start a Baptist church in Pahrump, Nevada, about fifty miles southwest of Las Vegas. Each had a heart for God and agreed that there was a need for more Baptist churches in Nevada.

We committed to support the first and third pastors at $500 a month for a period of two years. The second pastor, the one intending to start a Baptist church on the southwest side of Vegas, had been on our staff for a year. I asked him and his wife if they were both ready to start a new church after being on staff at Liberty for only a year. They said they were. I told them that we would pay the rent on their meeting place for the first year, along with his salary plus health insurance. I explained that after the first year we would continue to pay the rent and their salary at 50% of the first year. Several families from Liberty agreed to attend his new church and assist him in church matters. Members from our church helped renovate the new storefront church. Doors were knocked, people were invited, and things went well the first year.

It was an exciting time. We watched three different church plants begin to grow. The gentleman who pastored the Pahrump church eventually assumed an existing failing church. The church at that time was running thirty to fifty people. Today, it is a well established church running between 250–300 in a rural community. Although the church on the northwest side of town is still in a rented facility under a long-term lease, it too, has become well established. They are self supporting and God is blessing them.

The second church, the one in southwest Las Vegas, had a difficult time. After about five years of struggling, the pastor chose to dissolve the church. He subsequently moved to another state. There are three valuable lessons that can be learned from the failure of that church:

1. If the pastor of a mother church intends to send some of his members to assist the new pastor at the church plant, it is essential that those members of the mother church be 100 percent committed to establishing that new church.

2. Before agreeing to support the planting of a new church, the pastor of the mother church must make a comprehensive evaluation of the request and, if appropriate, summon the courage to articulate any unpleasant truths to someone looking for his support.

3. A good way to evaluate whether a pastor is ready to plant and pastor a new church is to give him an adult Bible study class and see if he can build it from a very few to fifty or sixty people. If he succeeds within a year or two, he likely will be able to establish a church.

In 2003, I learned of a gentleman and his family that lived in Kingman, Arizona, about one hundred miles from Las Vegas. He and his family joined our church. He explained that they traveled back and forth to be part of our services. I was impressed. After further conversations with him, he revealed that he had a degree in Bible and in Pastoral Theology from a well-respected college. He explained that he and his family did not attend church in Kingman because they couldn't find one they felt suited them.

"With your degree," I asked, "why don't you start one?"

He admitted that the idea had occurred to him, but he made no commitment. Sometime later he started a church in Kingman. He was also an independent businessman. Both his pastorate and business prospered for some time. His church grew quickly, but faced some difficulty due to competing demands on his time. It is difficult to pastor a church and to build a successful business at the same time. Subsequently, he brought in a couple of men to assume the pastorate, and he eventually resigned. In 2011, another young man came and is now pastoring the church fulltime. That church is struggling, particularly because Kingman is not a large community. However, I believe that with proper leadership and direction, a church can succeed in Kingman.

Shortly after the attack on the Twin Towers in New York, one of our missionaries who intended to go to Cuba and start a work was denied a visa because of security problems resulting from the 9/11 attack. He had a heart for Spanish-speaking people. He approached me about the possibility of starting a Baptist church for them in Las Vegas. I told him that I thought it was a great idea. Shortly thereafter, he started the Great Commission Baptist Church. We were already supporting him through our missions account, so he did not need any additional finances. That church is just about ready to have its own Spanish pastor.

People ask me how many churches we've planted in Las Vegas. The answer is one: Liberty Baptist Church. However, we have helped several others begin. By helping these churches start, we have studied what works and what doesn't. These many years have helped us to develop the philosophies and procedures you will read about in the following pages. Adopting these philosophies helped us in 2004 to successfully contribute to the planting of Southern Hills Baptist Church, which is discussed in the next chapter.

SIXTEEN

The Southern Hills
Baptist Church Story

In thirty-five years of ministry we have made many mistakes. However, I believe we have come to a point where we understand the dynamics of starting a New Testament Baptist church. When I say we have helped churches start, that means a variety of things.

When one pastor came to town, we sent over some church members to help him with doorknocking, nursery, and Sunday school teaching. We gave him $2,000 a month for the first three months to encourage him and then continued to support him for some time at $200 a month. We have helped churches by helping them locate facilities. We have printed tens of thousands of tracts for churches coming to the Las Vegas Valley. We have purchased baptismal pools and other equipment such as chairs, songbooks, and sound equipment. We helped one church by paying its rent and the pastor's salary for the first year. We supported two other churches for the first two years. I have come to the conclusion, however, that the best way to help a church get planted is the way we helped Southern Hills Baptist Church.

Southern Hills Baptist Church began on August 1, 2004. Two years before, Pastor Joshua Teis, my son, came to work for Liberty Baptist Church. He came with the intent of working as an intern for two years to gain experience in the ministry. He also came with the intent of planting a church somewhere in the Las Vegas Valley. Following is a step-by-step description of what he and his wife Heather did to begin the Southern Hills Baptist Church.

- They joined Liberty Baptist Church.
- We immediately put him in charge of our young adult Bible studies.
- He and Heather went doorknocking five days per week, Tuesday through Saturday, for Liberty Baptist Church— one hundred doors per day.
- He prepared our Summer Camping program—Camp Liberty—a twelve-week program.
- He and Heather worked with our children's ministry.
- He taught a young adult Bible study class.

His class started with six adults. After a year and a half, he had over sixty adults. After the first year of serving at Liberty, we began to look for a place for him to begin another independent Baptist church. When he was not performing specific duties at Liberty, he spent his time on the road looking for a place that God would have him plant a church. About six months before he was ready to start his church, we did a few things:

First, we located an empty warehouse on the far southwest part of the valley, about thirty minutes from Liberty. We made an offer to the leasing agent. The owner accepted the offer contingent on approval of a use permit from the county commission. We didn't foresee any problems. We put together a flyer, complete with the Gospel, telling people that a new church was coming to town. We wanted to mail or deliver it to 75,000 homes. I announced to the members at Liberty that we were going to plant a new church in the Las Vegas Valley.

Second, we made known to the members of Liberty that anyone wishing to help Pastor Joshua start the new church needed to apply for a specific position. The application was to be approved by Pastor Josh and myself. Our members were eager to help. Pastor Joshua added over sixty people to Liberty Baptist Church in the year and a half he interned there. He and Heather had earned our support. We did not want people going over to the new church plant unless they made a commitment to help Joshua and Heather in their work. Those whose applications we approved were told that they would each be designated as church planters.

Next, we turned our attention to raising financial support for the new plant. I made a list of pastor friends, and Joshua formulated a letter. We took pictures of the rented building, put together our plan, showed the need, and wrote letters to 75–100 pastors. During the following two months, we received support checks and promises of support. That was sufficient to help us pay for the first year's rent and Pastor Josh's salary. When I sent out the letter, I was able to tell these pastors that Joshua had proven himself to be a soulwinner, that he had built a Sunday school class from six to over sixty people, and that Liberty was sending several families with Joshua to the new church. Forty-three members went from our church to Southern Hills Baptist Church, and I was able to confidently say that I believed Joshua would be able to build it.

We had planned on leasing the building, but later learned that the owner was willing to sell it for just a few dollars more than the rent. We went to our bank, refinanced our note on Liberty Baptist Church, and purchased the building. As financial support came in, we remodeled the warehouse using volunteer labor. It was renovated to include a beautiful auditorium, two nurseries, four classrooms, a foyer, four bathrooms, and an efficient (interpreted: small) office. Our plan was to finish the building the last week of July and open the doors August 1, 2004.

Things were going smoothly until a city inspector noticed the drop ceiling. He informed us that it did not meet code for a commercial grade building and that we would have to modify it to receive our use permit. This meant that the building would not be ready for occupancy on August 1, 2004 because, without the permit, we could not run air conditioners. Las Vegas is normally over one hundred degrees in August. We went to the county; we went to the state; we did everything we could to talk to everyone that would listen about getting a temporary use permit so that we could turn on air conditioners and at least meet there. We had invited some 70,000 to attend the opening service. We did not know what we were going to do. The week before we were supposed move in, we worked and prayed intensely, but it was obvious we were not going to have air conditioning.

We decided, that for that week, we would change the Sunday school hour into a church service, and that the following hour we would have a second service to keep everyone in the same area. We were able to run electrical chords from the building next door to our building to power the air conditioning unit. We purchased fans and ran extension cords from neighboring buildings into the other rooms so that people could walk in, take a tour of the facilities in the heat, and then come into the service. That was the opening day. There were 268 people in the services, and one family trusted Christ as Saviour. It was an overcast day, which is unusual for Las Vegas at that time of year. However, the clouds helped keep the temperature down. Overall, it was a wonderful victory and, for the next six weeks, the new church met in facilities that were not quite complete.

The average attendance the first few weeks was somewhere between 80–90 people. Five years later, Southern Hills Baptist Church averaged between 280–300 people. Two years after the church moved into the warehouse, Southern Hills agreed to purchase the property from us. They received a bank loan and paid us $800,000 for the building so that they owed us nothing. Within six months of its opening, they were paying their mortgage and had repaid every dollar Liberty put into their ministry.

Southern Hills Baptist Church is a great example of how to plant a church in the 21st century. Find a mother church that will support you financially and help build your church. Then go out from that mother church and do a work for the glory of God! Liberty Baptist Church was so excited about the birth of this new church that everyone, including this pastor, wanted to attend. We had worked diligently and invested much to make this day a reality. We did everything we could to restrain our people from attending Southern Hills on its opening day because we did not want to hinder what God was doing in this new church plant. It is very important that you emphasize to the people in the mother church that, unless they are part of the church plant, it is best for them to stay faithful to their own church and pray for the new church plant.

To help our people with this, we had videos taken of the first services and shared them with our people the following Sunday evening. We also encouraged our people to stop by and attend an evening service in the weeks and months ahead. This was an encouragement to both them and the new church plant.

SEVENTEEN

The Role of a Mother Church

It is my prayer that as you start a church, your desire would be to become a mother church and lead churches in the same way you were established. Several things are essential if your goal is to become a mother church.

Make sure your church is ready to give birth. The mother church needs to be self supporting. It is a mistake to attempt to start a new church out of one that itself is still struggling. The mother church should have property and buildings. The mother church should have a base. The pastor and staff should be well supported. It is preferred that a mother church have at least 200 to 250 members before attempting to plant a new church. If you plan to send seed members to the new church, you need to be able to sustain the loss of those families.

Develop a two-year plan. This is not something you do overnight. The plan should address both short-term actions and long-term ones. Short-term aspects should address a number of points including church birth and growth through specific means. For example, what avenues will you employ to let people know that there's a new church coming to town? Typical ways include doorknocking, flyers, pulpit announcements by pastors of local churches, media spots, and specifically, the internet. The plan should list assumptions and discuss uncertainties, along with contingency plans. Identify specific goals and dates in the plan. This will allow you to measure your progress, identify problem areas, and make any necessary corrections. For longer-term concerns, you need a long-term vision. Proverbs 29:18 tells us that without vision, the people perish. Realize that your plan is a living document. If you do a good job, it will probably outlive you! Sometimes it will be necessary to make adjustments and set new goals. Begin your plan with the end in mind—the end being a self-supporting, self-governing, self-propagating, independent Baptist church.

Select an area of the city that needs a new independent Baptist church. One likely location in nearly all towns and cities is where there is new housing. However, God may call you to support planting a church in a different location, maybe in an urban area.

As the pastor of a mother church, begin to interview potential church planters. Find a young man who is willing to work under your authority for no less than two years. Make sure he has a teachable spirit, and that his wife understands the concept of full-time Christian ministry for both of them. Make sure you are comfortable with them and that they are comfortable with you and the work God is calling them to do. The young man who aspires to become the pastor of his own church should have a heart to see your mother church increase, as well as begin his new church.

Announce to the church that you have brought on a pastoral intern. Explain that he will only be with you for two years before he leaves to plant a new church he intends to pastor. It's probably not wise to announce the location since either of you might be led by the Lord to a location of greater spiritual need during his two-year internship.

Give him a place to host one of the following:

- An adult Bible study or Sunday school class
- An evening Bible study for people he leads to Christ
- A Wednesday evening Bible study group that meets at the church. This will encourage him to go door to door in the area where the new church is to be planted, lead people to Christ, and invite them to hear him speak and become acquainted.

Have him visit in the area where the new church is to be planted. He can do this two days per week, knock on one hundred doors per day, and tell people about his plans to start a church. He should tell them that he has started a Bible study in his mother church and invite them to be part of it. He should write down their names on a prospect sheet and contact them on a regular basis to invite them to his Bible study.

Let him build that Bible study from the few that you give him to sixty or more. This will allow him to develop a core that will be his church planting team.

One year before the intern intends to start his new church, the pastor of the mother church should announce to the members that the young man is ready to start his new church. The senior pastor should invite any who wish to go with him to the new church to contact him (the senior pastor) to discuss the matter.

Have the intern present his work to the church that Sunday evening. Let them see that this is something that you fully support. No one should mistake this for a church split. Neither is the new church a refuge for people who are angry or upset with the senior pastor.

Have applications ready for members who want to go to the new church. The applications should include their names, addresses, and specific jobs they would be interested in doing at the new church. They must look at themselves as church planters, not just people who are coming to a new church that is more conveniently located. You do not want people who are just looking for a "smaller church." These people will be dead weight. The pastor of the mother church and the new church should both approve each applicant.

The list of specific jobs at a new church includes:

- Ushers
- Sunday School Teachers
- Nursery workers
- Adult Bible Study Teachers
- Janitors
- Greeters
- Decoration Coordinators (flowers/grounds/etc.)
- Parking lot attendants
- Piano players
- Youth workers

Six months prior to opening day, the volunteers should begin meeting to discuss specifically what they plan to do and finalize the organizational structure, along with roles and responsibilities. The attitude and enthusiasm expressed in these meetings should be similar to that of a pep rally.

Six months before the new church opens, the volunteers should start visiting in the area of the new church, having their lives centered around helping the new church begin. They should work alongside the pastor and his wife to develop a great opening Sunday.

The Sunday before the new church holds its first service, the pastor of the mother church should have the families that are going to the new church come forward in the service and have the men of the church gather around the group and pray collectively for the new church plant, sending them to this new mission work that is about to begin with their blessing and God's.

On opening Sunday, the intern-turned-pastor should have everything in place. Your nursery workers, your Sunday school teachers, a map of where the classes are to begin, and your ushers should be ready to greet people and bring them into the services. If possible, get a singing group from a solid fundamental Baptist college to sing. During the announcements, he should announce that that evening, the church will begin a four-day meeting— Sunday night, Monday night, Tuesday night, and Wednesday night. For that four-day meeting, you should have an experienced pastor come to preach, possibly the pastor of the mother church. Members from the mother church should come to help fill the seats so that guests will not feel as though they are part of an empty church. The church plant volunteers should welcome new visitors and make them feel at home. Each night a different aspect of the importance of the local church should be emphasized, along with the Gospel. (See Appendix D for topics and outlines.)

Each night the pastor should emphasize being back for the next Sunday morning service and bringing friends. Thursday and Friday of that first week should be dedicated to visiting the first-time guests. The pastor should visit the guests in their homes or at least call to reconnect one more time before the second service.

The purpose of the follow-up visits are threefold:

1. To allow the visitor to become personally acquainted with the pastor and his wife. These visits will allow you to interact on an intimate level that cannot be reached in the public arena of the local church.

2. Explain the direction, vision and ministries available for everyone in this new church plant.

3. You will have the opportunity to lead the visitor to Christ if they are not already saved, and to discuss baptism and church membership with them if they are already saved.

Now that the church has begun, the pastor must divide his time. A good schedule is:

- Morning—personal devotions and message preparation
- Afternoons and evenings—visiting
- Saturday—follow-up visitations

The goal of the new pastor is to strengthen the base and get all of the church planters to befriend as many of the visitors as possible. It should be explained to every member that has transferred from the mother church that their role and responsibility is to recruit as many new families as they possibly can. In attending a new church, the mature believer must realize that he has a heavy responsibility to help develop this church into the outreach center that God wants it to be. He will do that most effectively through his involvement in door-to-door soulwinning and personal follow up with visiting families.

EIGHTEEN

The Power of the Gospel

The greatest thing about starting an independent Baptist church is seeing lives changed through the power of the Gospel. My wife and I have had the privilege of knocking on thousands of doors in the Las Vegas Valley. We have had many wonderful experiences.

I recall one time as we went door to door, we knocked on the door of a man who was quite hostile. I invited him to visit Liberty Baptist Church and he responded, "I don't go to church. I'm an atheist."

To that, I responded, "Oh, you can't be an atheist. You are too intelligent to be an atheist."

He promptly replied, "What do you mean by that?"

I told him, "The Bible says, 'The fool hath said in his heart, There is no God.'

He looked at me somewhat puzzled and said, "Well, I guess I'm not really an atheist. I just don't know what to believe about God."

My wife and I had the privilege of briefly giving him the Gospel. As far as I know he did not receive Christ that day, but we did have the opportunity of planting the seed.

One very memorable door we knocked on belonged to Buck and Glenda. It was memorable for two reasons. When the door was opened, we saw inside the living room a Harley Davidson motorcycle. I must have looked somewhat stunned, but then I began to compliment him on his motorcycle. Buck bragged about his motorcycle a little bit, and I invited both Buck and Glenda to come to church. Buck didn't seem to be too interested, but Glenda was. The first Sunday that we opened the doors of our church, Glenda came and she brought a friend named Vicki, who lived right down the street from her. On that first Sunday morning, Glenda and Vicki both trusted Jesus Christ as their Lord and Saviour. God did a wonderful work in their lives. They continued to come to church. Their children trusted Christ as their Saviour. Las Vegas is a very transient community, and within the first year of our church both Glenda and Vicki moved out of town, but I know I will see them both in Heaven.

As I just stated, Las Vegas is very transient, and for that reason attendance at Liberty Baptist Church has grown and declined over the years. Anytime we went into a period of decline my wife and I would determine that we were just going to go out and knock on more doors. About six years after the church was established we hit a down time; finances were low and attendance was dropping. I had two options; one was to get more aggressive in the area of doorknocking or to go out and get a secular job. I remembered a book I read by John R. Rice that talked about his church planting efforts. He said when he was discouraged from a lack of results of doorknocking that he would just keep doing what God told him to do, knowing that God wrote his paycheck. I determined it would be more effective to knock on doors eight hours a day than it would be to work a secular job eight hours a day.

On one particular occasion my wife and I knocked on the door of a sixteen-year-old young man. In the front of his house sat a DeLorean, the same type of car that was used in the movie *Back to the Future*. Chris Smith came to the door that day. We asked him if he knew for sure if he died right then he would go to Heaven.

Chris said, "No." He had never heard that you could know. We shared with him how Jesus Christ suffered and died, paid the penalty of his sin, was buried and three days later rose from the dead, having paid for his sin. He bowed his head on the doorstep and trusted Jesus Christ as his Lord and Saviour. Chris began to come to church on a regular basis. He later brought his brother Bill. Bill later trusted Jesus Christ as his Lord and Saviour. Eventually Chris married a young lady from our youth department named Lenaya. He and Lenaya moved to Virginia where they attended Bible college. He is serving as a youth director in Virginia today. He has a wonderful family and all of his children love the Lord and are serving Him. The Gospel truly does transform lives.

One day a gentleman came to me and said, "Pastor, will you visit my friend, Don Kroll? I have invited him to church but he just won't come. I told him you would stop by."

Within the week I stopped by his home. I knocked on his front door. When he opened the door he said, "What do you want?" He honestly looked as if he were angry at the world.

I told him that his friend Tom had asked me to stop by and visit with him, and that I was the pastor of Liberty Baptist Church. I introduced my wife, and he invited us to come in. He motioned us into the living room and asked me to have a seat. A fellow like Don, not interested in small talk, looked at me and said, "So what did Tom want you to talk to me about?"

I very simply looked at him and said, "Well, Don, since you asked, I have come over here to share with you what the Bible says about how you can know for sure you are going to Heaven. Has anybody ever shared that with you?"

His response was a direct, "No."

I said, "Could I share with you what the Bible says?"

With the same unhappy look in his face he said, "Yes."

I opened the Bible and shared with him the Gospel of Jesus Christ. How Jesus loved him, suffered and died to pay the penalty for his sin. How He was buried and three days later arose from the dead, having paid for his sin. I told him we are all sinners and need to put our faith and trust in Him for salvation. I asked him if the Gospel made sense to him and he said again, "Yes."

I said, "I could lead you in a prayer right now, and you can trust Jesus Christ as your Lord and Saviour. Would you like to do that?" I was almost sure that he would say no, and I was ready to shake his hand and walk out the door.

To my surprise he said, "Yes, I would like that."

We bowed our heads, and I lead him in the sinner's prayer. When it was finished I looked at him and he looked at me and had the biggest smile I have ever seen on anyone's face. He told me he didn't know it was that simple. I invited him to church, and he said he would love to come. That following week he brought his wife Mary with him to church. Mary said to me, "I don't know what happened to Don. The night you came to our house he went to the liquor cabinet and poured all his liquor down the kitchen sink. There has been a huge change in his life." Mary trusted Christ as her Lord and Saviour as well.

Tom and Marlene came to visit our church by the invitation of her friend. Though Tom had gone to several churches in town, he had never heard a plain Gospel presentation. After attending for three weeks he came forward and said to a counselor, "I have been coming here for the last three weeks and the preacher keeps saying you can know for sure you are going to Heaven. I want to know how."

Our counselors took both him and his wife to the back, shared with them how Christ suffered and died for them, how He was buried and rose from the dead to pay for their sin, and that they could call on Christ. They both trusted Jesus Christ as their Lord and Saviour. Both of them were baptized in Lake Mead. They both went through our discipleship training. Tom has been our soundman for probably the last twenty-five years.

John and Jan Shorer came to our church after trusting in Jesus Christ as Lord and Saviour at another church about forty miles away. When they were invited to Liberty and came the first time they said, "This place is way too radical for us."

They went from church to church. Finally, they decided to give Liberty one more try. The following week, I had the opportunity to go by and visit with them in their home. They were both teachers in the public school system. In fact, he was an award-winning band director in the state of Nevada. They asked several questions and let us know frankly, that they would probably not be back again, but they continued to come. Another couple in our church, Kyle and Kamie Haynes, began to reach out to them and befriend them.

They were baptized and became members of Liberty Baptist Church. After a while, knowing about his educational degree, I approached him about the possibility of helping us start a Christian school. I told him that I would like to personally disciple him over the next several months. Those several months turned into two years, but at the end of those two years John was ready to come on staff and help us begin Liberty Baptist Academy. He is our associate pastor, and he has worked with our children's ministry, directs our choir, has led our music, and has faithfully served as principal for Liberty Baptist Academy for the past fourteen years.

From 1999 until 2009, our church was in a continual state of growth and building. During that time we had several building superintendents, most of them from Liberty Baptist Church. However, when we began our auditorium expansion we hired an outside construction firm. The construction superintendent for that firm was a gentleman named Kurt Braneff. Kurt is a tall, outspoken Texan whose mannerisms would remind you of John Wayne. From the first time I met Kurt I knew I liked him, and we constantly invited Kurt to visit our church. When it came time to dedicate our auditorium, I invited him and his family to come to the dedication service. They came. Then they came to an old-fashioned themed service, our big day, where we gave the Gospel very clearly and plainly. At the end of that service, both he and his wife raised their hands to trust Jesus Christ as Lord and Saviour. Linda, his wife, came up afterwards and said she had been going to church for over fifty years and had never heard the Gospel in a clear, easy-to-understand way. Soon after that, Kurt and Linda were baptized and have served faithfully in our church ever since. My wife and I had the privilege of taking Kurt and Linda along with another faithful couple through discipleship for about six or eight months. Kurt is a faithful choir member and is now becoming more and more involved in personal ministry and visitation outreach.

One afternoon, a young lady walked into our office with her teenage son who lived not far from the church. She was very concerned and asked if she could see the pastor. She and her teenage son came into my office and she began to share with me her concerns. Her teenage boy in a public school had written a suicide note and had also threatened to take the life of a young woman in the school. I talked to the young man about life and the importance of knowing for sure he was going to Heaven. He trusted Christ as his Lord and Saviour that day. He and his mother started attending church. He then brought his brothers, and his father soon began to attend as well. It wasn't long until their entire family and extended family were attending Liberty Baptist Church. All of them trusted Christ as their Lord and Saviour. He and one of his brothers both attended West Coast Baptist College. His other brother attended Pensacola Christian College. One of his brothers is now in full-time Christian ministry. His family members are all faithful members of Liberty Baptist Church. These are just a few of the stories of lives being changed at Liberty.

Several years ago a young man said to me, "Don't you think doorknocking is a little passé?" All I know is that when we faithfully go doorknocking and tell people about Christ, God faithfully brings people to our doors, and we have the opportunity of seeing people get saved. Over the last thirty-five years we have seen the Gospel of Jesus Christ change lives, and it is still changing lives today.

"It's easier to birth a baby than it is to raise the dead." Tell that to the woman who has been in labor for twenty-four hours, and you might get an argument. That, however, was the advice that I was given when I was encouraged to start a church from scratch. Birthing a church is no easy task. It will take long hours and much personal sacrifice. You will be criticized for what you do and what you don't do. Some will call you liberal; some will call you a legalist. There will be people who say you don't care; others will tell you that you care too much. There will be times of introspection where you compare yourself with other ministries that are either doing better or worse than you. Second Corinthians 10:12 says, "For we dare not make ourselves of the number, or compare ourselves with some that commend themselves: but they measuring themselves by themselves, and comparing themselves among themselves, are not wise." You will know it is not wise, but you will do it anyway. Planting a church will take all your energy and your effort. You will have to be a person who is determined and one who has a passion to accomplish the task.

If that is the case, why would you want to be part of starting a church? Let me give you several reasons:

- The church of Jesus Christ is God's ordained institution for reaching our world today.
- It is the greatest movement on planet Earth.
- It is the representation of God's kingdom here on Earth.
- The Bible says the gates of Hell will not stop it from moving forward.

It is a privilege to be able to be a part of planting a New Testament Baptist church. If God calls you to plant a church, you are among the honored few.

Every night, no matter what the circumstances, you can thank God that you have the privilege of being a part of what He is doing in your city, your state, and around the world. You will have the great reward of watching people's lives changed. You will see people who were heading to Hell receive Christ and are now heading to Heaven, religious people become truly converted, and families molded to bring glory and honor to God. After many years of struggle you will be able to sit back and look at all that God has done in and through your life.

I read a quote from Bill Rice, the founder of the Bill Rice Ranch, that said, "If it was easy everybody would be doing it." That may be the reason we don't have too many church planters in our culture today. Remember that great reward comes with great sacrifice; great victories come from great battles. When you march into Satan's domain and say you are going to plant a church for the glory of Jesus Christ, you can expect opposition; but you also have the Lord Jesus Christ, your captain, and the head of His church on your side. If you keep fighting the battles, proclaiming the truth, and moving forward by faith you will see great victories, great results, and the great reward of someday hearing the words of our Lord Jesus Christ, "Well done, thou good and faithful servant."

In my office, above my desk, I have a plaque that was given to me many years ago. It reads, "Commitment is what transforms a promise into reality." It is those words that speak boldly of our intentions and actions which speak louder than words. It is making time when there is none—coming through time after time, and year after year.

Commitment is the stuff character is made of, the power of change in the face of things. It is the daily triumph of integrity over skepticism. If God calls you to plant a church, follow His lead with passion. Make a commitment to stay where God plants you, and get ready for one exciting life serving God in the greatest institution on earth, His church. May God bless you as you serve Him.

Are You a Gospel Preacher?

Make sure you are a Gospel preacher. Many claim to preach the Gospel. The sad thing is that many do not even know the Gospel. I attended the funeral of a close friend not too long ago. The pastor of the church was a godly man. He said over and over again, "I know that my friend is in Heaven. That's because he was saved, and he would want each of you to be saved. I hope that today you will trust Christ and be saved." Over and over he stressed the importance of being saved. He talked about the glories of Heaven. He explained the agony of Hell, but he never told people how to get saved. He never gave the Gospel. Make sure when you say you are going to give the Gospel that you *give the Gospel*. What exactly is the Gospel?

Paul introduces the Gospel in 1 Corinthians 15:1, "Moreover, brethren, I declare unto you the gospel...." He gives us the Gospel beginning in verse 3, "For I delivered unto you first of all that which I also received, how that Christ died for our sins according to the scriptures; And that he was buried, and that he rose again the third day according to the scriptures: And that he was seen of Cephas, then of the twelve: After that, he was seen of above five hundred brethren at once...."

Charles Ryrie, of the Ryrie Study Bible, identifies in this passage two proclamations and two proofs. The first proclamation is that Christ died for our sins. The proof is that He was buried. The second proclamation is that Jesus rose from the dead. The proof is He was seen by hundreds. The Gospel is that Jesus Christ died for our sins; it is not that He died for us. There are soldiers throughout history that have died for us. Jesus did not just die for us, He died for our sins. He paid the penalty of our sins in our place on the cross. This is a very important part of the Gospel, but that is not where it ends.

Some preachers say, "Christ died for you!" These, like the Roman Catholic Church, leave Christ dead on the cross. The Gospel is not just that Christ died for our sins and was buried. The fact that He rose from the dead after paying for our sins is proof that He is God! But, His resurrection was not in stealth. The Bible affirms that He was seen by hundreds of people. That is proof. We do not see spirits. He was seen in the flesh by over five hundred eyewitnesses.

Friend, if you are going to share the Gospel, if you are going to write a Gospel tract, if you are going to give out Gospel tracts, make *sure* that the Good News, the Gospel message, is included! Often I pick up a copy of the Romans Road that does not have the Gospel in it. I listen to "Gospel" messages that do not have the Gospel in them. When you prepare a brochure for your church, make sure the Gospel is included. I have included exactly what we put as our short Gospel message on the back of every tract. You will note that it tells the Good News—that Christ suffered and died, paid the penalty of our sin, was buried, and rose from the dead having paid for our sin. It gives readers an opportunity to pray and trust Jesus Christ and what He did for them by paying their sin debt.

I have also included the Gospel presentation that we teach our members to give in Appendix B—Five Things We Must Know and One Thing We Must Do to Be Saved. It burdens my heart that we live in an age when most do not know the truth of the Word of God. Our world believes in a Jesus, but not the Jesus of the Bible. Several years ago, I came to the conclusion that it is imperative that when we present the Gospel message, we let people know exactly what we believe.

Below is an example of the Gospel we place on our tracts:

You Can Know for Sure You Are Going to Heaven

We all know that we are not perfect and that one day we will stand before a righteous God to give an account for our lives. At that moment, you can be sure that you will enter Heaven if you simply put your trust in these truths:

Jesus Christ, God in human flesh, paid the penalty for our sins by dying on the cross (Romans 5:8). He was buried, and three days later He rose from the dead proving that He is God (1 Corinthians 15:3–4). He now offers all who put their trust in Him free access into Heaven through His death, burial, and resurrection (Romans 10:13).

If you call on Jesus, admit your sin, ask Him to give you eternal life, and trust only in Him and not your good works, you can be sure of Heaven. I hope you do that today!

You can pray this simple prayer:

"Lord Jesus, I know that I'm a sinner. I know that you are God and that you died to pay for my sins. I believe that you rose from the dead, proving that you are God. Right now, in the best way I know how, I ask you to be my Lord, my Saviour, and my God. Thank you, Jesus, for dying for me. Help me now to live for you. Amen."

Five Things We Must Know and One Thing We Must Do to Be Saved

We teach that there are five things a person must know and one thing he must do to get to Heaven.

1. The Bible is the Word of God (2 Timothy 3:16; 2 Peter 1:21).

2. Jesus Christ is the God of the Bible (Isaiah 9:6; Isaiah 7:14; John 1:1; John 14:9; Revelation 1:8). The Jesus of the Jehovah Witnesses, the Jesus of the Latter-Day Saints, the Jesus of our pop culture is not God. Many so-called churches today teach that He was a good man, a prophet, or an angel. However, such a Jesus would not have the power to save. The Jesus of the Bible is God in human flesh. We must explain that He is the God-man, fully God and at the same time fully man.

3. We are all sinners (Romans 3:10; Romans 3:23). We are all in the same boat. We never point a finger at someone else. We understand that we're all sinners.

4. Because of our sin, we are separated from God and will inhabit Hell for all eternity unless we put our trust in the Jesus of the New Testament for salvation (Romans 6:23; Romans 5:12). We all deserve to go to Hell, but Jesus Christ, God in human flesh, paid our sin debt on Calvary for the penalty of our sin.

5. Jesus paid for our sin by dying on Calvary's cross and rising from the dead so that sinful men could be reconciled to a Holy God (Romans 5:8). He was buried, and three days later He rose from the dead and was seen by hundreds. Now, He is in Heaven, and there is only one thing we must do in order to spend eternity with Him.

What one thing must we do to be saved? We must personally put our faith and trust in Him and what He did for us and call upon Him, asking Him to be our Lord, Saviour, and God (Romans 10:9–10). The Bible assures us in Romans 10:13, "For whosoever shall call upon the name of the Lord shall be saved." This is the Gospel. Make sure, as a Gospel preacher, that you always include the Gospel in every message you preach!

Why Some Churches Fail

I used to think that just about anyone could start a church. Experience has taught me otherwise. I have seen many churches start. Some have been successful and others, not so much. Ultimately God adds to the church (Acts 2:47), but He uses Spirit-filled people as His tools. If you desire to plant a church, you and your wife must have certain character qualities.

1. You must love people. That does not mean that people do not get on your nerves or irritate you from time to time, but you must be one who loves to be with people, people from all backgrounds, people of all kinds. People will know if you are using them to build a ministry. Years ago, Jack Hyles said, "You should never use your people to build your ministry, but you should use your ministry to

build your people." It is absolutely essential that you love people and that you care about them. The Lord's work is all about people. It's not about programs. It's not about being a big shot. It's about loving and caring for people. Keep loving others even when they don't love you, and you will eventually reap what you sow. If you don't love people, don't start a church.

2. You must preach well. When you start a church, one thing you're going to need that will keep people coming back is good preaching. This means you must study. It means you must have a good grasp of the king's English. It means you must be somewhat educated. It means you must have a teachable spirit and be able to be reproved when you say or do something wrong. A preacher should listen to himself preach. Often when we get a good dose of ourselves, we will make changes we need to make. You must preach well.

3. You must be a hard worker. You have to be self motivated. No one is going to make you get up in the morning. No one is going to make you stay up late at night. You must be someone who is willing to work long and hard without appreciation and often times with major criticism. After you've worked eighty or ninety hours a week, some guy will say to you, "I wish I only had to work three hours a week." You must stay calm. Most are just pulling your chain.

You may wish to respond in some instances with, "You're right! I need to preach much longer sermons." You must enjoy doing the work you do. You must be determined to knock on doors when it's hot, when it's cold, and even when it's raining. Your perspiration will fill the pews, and that is all that will fill them.

4. You must have drive. You must have a passion. You must be driven, not to the point where you break your priorities or violate Bible principles, but you must be driven. There must be a passion in you to want to succeed and to want to build a church for Christ.

5. You must be persistent. You must determine, "I am not going to quit no matter WHAT happens. I will not give up on this. God has called me to this, and I am going to stay." There will be ups and downs in your ministry. Some days you will be flying, some years you will be flying. Others, it will level off. You may have a time when your attendance drops and you will want to call it quits. You must be persistent and say, "I am here for the long haul."

Here are several reasons why some churches fail:

1. Preachers forget that there is a difference between shepherds and sheep. If sheep naturally did that which was right, there would be no need for the shepherd. God ordained the pastorate because people are like sheep

who go astray. You must not let the wandering sheep, the disobedient ones, the ignorant cause you to want to quit. You must decide that you are going to keep on going.

2. The wife of the pastor will not be involved. She is involved with her children, she is at home nesting, she is working a secular job, and she is generally disinterested in the ministry. A church planting pastor needs his wife by his side. A woman that visits the church with her husband and sees that the pastor's wife is not there will soon say, "Let's go somewhere else." The pastor's wife is key, especially in the early years of the church. Churches fail because the pastor's wife is not involved.

3. The pastor will not go soulwinning or gets distracted from the main thing, which is teaching and preaching and winning people to Christ. Discipleship is not playing golf with a church member. Discipleship is hard work. Lazy pastors will not succeed. It is your job to knock on doors. It is your job to develop messages that are relevant, interesting, and that challenge your people to do the right things. Your wife and your children will always be your priority. That does not mean that your ministry should lack. If you have the desire to take it easy most of the time, then don't plant a church.

4. Bad preaching. It is difficult to overcome bad preaching, but in order to do so, you must have a teachable spirit.

Many other obstacles can be improved, but a pastor's preaching is personal, and any criticism of his speaking ability can be offensive. Nevertheless, you need to understand this truth, if someone comes to your church and does not come back, it is because they do not feel loved or they don't feel they are getting fed the Word of God. You need to have meat in your messages for mature believers, milk for new believers, and you need to make your presentation interesting and effective for all believers. Be willing to listen as people critique your messages. I have said this before, but it bears repeating, listen to yourself preach. When someone tries to help you with your preaching style, do not take offence. Listen and let God grow you as a communicator. Determine to become effective in your presentation. If being excited in the pulpit is not your "cup of tea," then don't start a church. If you don't like to dig in the Word of God for nuggets that make the message interesting, then don't start a church. Pastoring people means motivating them to do what is right, and they cannot be motivated if they are bored with your messages. My homiletics teacher, Dr. Earl Miller, used to say, "It's a sin to be boring." I couldn't agree more.

5. Self-will and an unteachable spirit result when a pastor thinks he knows it all and has nothing to learn. He cannot be helped by anyone, not by another pastor, not by any

other members of the church. Often a loving member will come to him and say, "Pastor, I think we need to change something." An arrogant pastor will reply, "I don't need any help from you, and you can just go someplace else." He may resist what God is trying to teach him through a loving member. If a pastor is self-willed and will not listen to the advice of anyone else, then he will fail. It may take a while, but he will not make it, and the church will not succeed.

The church planting pastor must be friendly, must love people, must have his wife and children 100 percent involved in the ministry, must be willing to work hard, get up early and stay up late, protect his family, work as hard to serve his family as his church, pray like mad, and preach with such a passion as though the salvation of lost souls depends completely on him. He must remember always that he represents God and that this is God's church, not his. When a church planting pastor applies these truths to his life and ministry, he will have the power and presence of God in his ministry, and he will be a success.

Suggested Outlines for the First Four Meetings

Why God Began the Local Church

Introduction: Matthew 16:18

Jesus said, "I will build My church." God established three institutions.

1. The Family—Genesis 2
2. The Government—Genesis 9
3. The Local Church—Matthew 16:18

Each of these were given to benefit the members: the family to mature and grow; the government to protect and defend; the local church to proclaim God's truth to the world, provide for God's sheep and to promote God's Kingdom.

I.   To Proclaim God's Truth to the World

    A.   Luke 19:10—we are to reach the lost

        1.   Door to door

        2.   Friend to friend

   B.   Matthew 28:19–20—Make Disciples

        1.   We are to disciple.

        2.   We are to baptize the saved.

        3.   We are to teach the Word.

II.   To Provide for God's Sheep—Acts 2:41–47

   A.   The apostle's doctrine

   B.   Fellowship

   C.   Breaking of bread and baptism

   D.   Prayer

   E.   Praise

III.   To Promote the Kingdom of God—Acts 1:8

   A.   The local church is to send out missionaries.

   B.   The local church is called to be light and salt
       —Matthew 5:13–16

   C.   The local church is to be the pillar and ground of truth
       —1 Timothy 3:15

Conclusion: The purpose of this new church is to:

   A.   Proclaim God's truth.

   B.   Provide for God's sheep.

   C.   Promote God's kingdom.

You and Your Church

Introduction: Read Ephesians 4:1–15

How does the church operate? Why do we come to church, and what is my role?

I.   God Provides Spiritual Leadership—v. 11

    A.   Apostles—The Word of God

    B.   Prophets—Preachers

    C.   Evangelists—Soulwinners

    D.   Pastors and Teachers

II.   God Wants Saints To Grow—v. 12

    A.   For the perfecting of the saints

    B.   *Perfecting* means "maturing"

    C.   As the men of God preach the Word of God, Christians grow in the Word

    D.   As they grow, they do:

        1.   The work of the ministry

        2.   The building of the body

III.   God Wants a Stable Church—v.14

    A.   Where proper doctrine is preached

    B.   Where the proper spirit is maintained

    C.   Where a proper balance is promoted

The church will be filled with stable people and stable families.

Conclusion:

God has given you this church. In order for it to be stable, the preacher must preach the truth; the saints must grow with the truth, and the entire body must practice the truth. And God will get the glory.

What Is a Real Church

Introduction: Matthew 7:15–21

The Bible is very clear that in the last days there will be false prophets in our world. Today, many organizations call themselves the church of God, but they are not. Jesus said, "…I will build my church; and the gates of hell shall not prevail against it." That church Jesus said He would build must be in the world today. Therefore, how do we identify it so we do not get led away by false doctrine?

I.   God's People—Philippians 1:1

In Philippians 1:1 there are three categories of people named in the church:

A.   The saints—all the believers

B.   Bishops—the term *bishop* is synonymous with two other terms used in Scripture. They are the leaders in the church and are referred to by three different titles.

1.   Bishops—Overseers /managers

2.   Elders—Mature believers

3.   Pastors—Shepherds /care-givers

C.   Deacons

      1.   Servants in the church

      2.   They help the pastor serve the people.

The local church must have the proper people.

II.   God's Doctrine—Acts 2:42

   A.   The Doctrines of Christ

      1.   His Deity

      2.   His Virgin Birth

      3.   His Death, Burial, and Resurrection

   B.   The Doctrine of the Bible

      1.   Inspired

      2.   Inerrant

      3.   Preserved

   C.   The Doctrine of Salvation by Grace through Faith Alone

      1.   Saved by grace—Ephesians 2:8–9

      2.   Eternally secure—Romans 8:28–39

   D.   The Doctrine of the Church

      1.   Local

      2.   Visible

      3.   Autonomous/Self-governing

   E.   The Doctrine of Baptism

      1.   After salvation

      2.   Into the body

   F.   The Doctrine of the Second Coming

      1.   Pre-tribulational

      2.   Pre-millennial

III. God's Practice—Romans 12:1–2

   A.   The church and its members are not to look like the world.

   B.   We are ambassadors of Christ—2 Corinthians 5:20.

   C.   We are to be holy—1 Peter 1:14–16.

Conclusion:

A real church will:

   1.   Be filled with God's people.

   2.   Teach God's doctrine.

   3.   Practice God's truth.

What God Wants from His Church

Introduction: 1 Thessalonians 2:13–17

Now that we understand why God began the local church, how we fit in the local church, and what we believe and why, tonight we will examine what God expects from His church.

I.   A Saved Church—v.13

   A.   Every member should be saved.

   B.   Make sure everyone knows how to be saved—give the Gospel.

II. A Sanctified Church

   A.   Believers should live lives set apart to God.

   B.   All Christians should live holy lives.

III. A Shining Church—v.14

The glory of Christ should shine from your life.

IV. A Standing Fast Church—v.15

   A.   We do not need to be like the world.

   B.   We do not need to look like the world to reach the world.

V. A Sharing Christ Church

Holding the traditions

   A.   We are ambassadors—2 Corinthians 5:20.

   B.   We live our testimony.

      1.   1 Thessalonians 5:14–24

      2.   We win souls.

      3.   We send missionaries.

Conclusion:

This new church needs to realize we are His church, and we must live to represent Him in all we do.

EPILOGUE
BY MATTHEW TEIS

We were privileged to grow up in the home of Dave and Anna Teis. Most people agree that Las Vegas, Nevada, is not the ideal place to raise a Christian family, but for me, my sisters, and brother Las Vegas is home and a great place to learn the Bible, represent the Saviour, and apply practical Christianity.

This book holds the story of how our parents, by the grace of God, founded the Liberty Baptist Church. We witnessed this miracle happen firsthand. We know it is the desire of our dad for this book to challenge its reader by the illustrations and stories, but most of all learn that our God, the Lord Jesus Christ, is able to overcome any obstacle that planting a church presents.

We understand that our dad is not perfect and may even change some of the things that he did in his ministry, but one thing remains the same about our dad from the earliest days of ministry to now. He is real. His walk with God is not some manufactured reality. He genuinely walks with God.

I remember watching him read the Bible when no one was around, when we were present, and when he was in public. He prays. He does not just talk about waking up at 5 AM to pray. He really does. He does not just talk about the need to witness. He shares the Gospel at every opportunity. He does not just theorize about the importance of the family. He deliberately invests himself in the life of his wife and five children. This is not just a book by someone who researched the best way to do something. This book is the manual that formed our church and shaped our lives.

All of our parents' children demonstrate a genuine desire for the Lord. I am now the executive pastor of Liberty Baptist Church and have served there for nearly twelve years. Josh founded Southern Hills Baptist Church on the southern edge of Las Vegas nearly eight years ago. Our sisters Charity, Faith, and Hope (yes, those are their real names) serve at Liberty in various capacities, with Hope graduating from West Coast Baptist College in the Spring of 2012.

We hope that this story challenges you to pursue God's plan for you with reckless abandon. There are no exaggerations in these covers. The people are real. We went to Sunday school with them, waited late into the night at Denny's for our parents to finish talking to them, and witnessed the transformation in their lives that only God can perform. I pray the story of our parents' obedience to Jesus Christ has encouraged you to find hope for your hometown.

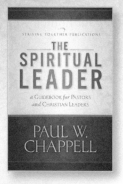
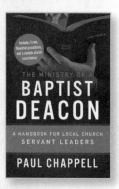

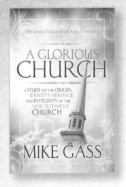
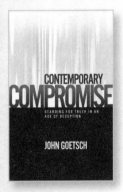

Visit us online

strivingtogether.com

wcbc.edu